Property Investment: Create Your Own Legacy

Simon Tim Muwanguzi

Copyright © Simon Tim Muwanguzi 2017

Published by Powerhouse Publications

All rights reserved. The author asserts their moral right under the Copyright, Designs and Patents Act 1988 to be identified as the author of this work.

Except for the quotation of small passages for the purposes of criticism and review, no part of this publication may be reproduced, stored in a retrieval system, or transmitted, in any form or by any means, electronic, mechanical, photocopying, recording or otherwise, except under the terms of the Copyright, Designs and Patents Act 1988 without the prior consent of the publisher.

This book is dedicated to our "special" daughter,

Kirsty Muwanguzi

www.timoseks.com

Contents

Foreword vii

Introduction 9

Chapter 1: Laying the Foundations: *What is Property Investment?* 23

Chapter Two: Dream Big Dreams: *When and Why Invest in Properties* 37

Chapter 3: Knowledge is Power: *Mortgages, Buy-to-Let, and Commercial Finance* 49

Chapter 4: Seeing the Big Picture: *How to Invest in Properties* 71

Chapter 5: Making the Right Choices About the Ideal Type of Property to Buy: *Residential and Commercial Properties. Does Size Matter?* 83

Chapter 6: Sowing the Seeds and Reaping the Rewards: *How does one make shrewd property investments?* 105

Chapter 7: Where There's a Will, There's a Way: *Overcoming Obstacles to Making Money From Property Investment.* 123

Chapter 8: Failure is Not an Option – Winner Takes All: *Property Investment Options and Solutions* 137

Chapter 9: He Who Dares, Wins: *My Personal Journey and Thoughts* 153

A Glossary of Property Terms 173

A List of Useful Contacts 183

Acknowledgements 187

Foreword

Creating wealth is the one thing that seems to be what the majority of people want to do – yet they struggle with this seemingly simple thing.

When Simon Tim Sekagya Muwanguzi decided to leave his native homeland of Uganda and move to London 20 years ago, that was the main thing on his mind. He knew that there was more to life and he wanted to go there to learn the tricks of the property trade, and then bring this back to his homeland to share with his fellow countrymen to help them to achieve the same success that he enjoys.

Having failed many times, Simon knew that consistency, determination, dedication and the "never give up attitude" were the traits he needed to achieve his goals. Life is not always easy.

However, by applying the aforementioned values, he knew everything was possible.

Now, Simon has put pen to paper to share his knowledge with you. This book is a simple and concise guide to show you how you can achieve wealth and success in the property arena. As with many things in life, they go up and down. The difference with property investment is that it may have slumps, but it always appreciates in value over time.

What Simon will teach you is how you can also achieve what he has been able to do and become a master in the property game.

You will soon discover that you can do this too, with the same traits and knowledge that Simon has applied.

– Clare Turner-Marshall.

Introduction

I am writing this book to share with you my experience and knowledge about the real estate industry, particularly regarding property investment and mortgages. The book is for anyone who wishes to know the basics about how to achieve wealth through investing in properties. As you may gather from the content in the following chapters, there are some real-life examples and case studies which, if applied promptly, will enable you to become not only very successful but also create your own legacy through something you are really passionate about.

As an immigrant from Uganda who has lived in London for the last 20 years, working as a property and mortgage consultant for over ten years, I do believe that by sharing the knowledge that I now have, you may not only receive more insight into how the real estate industry operates, but also become empowered and motivated to start your own journey of making serious money from property investment. I hope that you will eventually become a property tycoon with a multi-million property portfolio, either here in the UK or anywhere else in the world. As you may gather, most of the content in this book is related to circumstances or scenarios here in the UK, but since the dynamics of the real estate industry are similar, the ideas and suggestions mentioned are relevant to any reader worldwide.

Basically, the principles of buying a property for commercial gain are quite similar wherever you are on earth. If you are a cash buyer, you may instruct your lawyers to prepare the necessary documents to purchase the property of your choice outright. On the other hand, if you need a mortgage to buy the property, you shall be required to provide proof of identity, address, and income to the bank or mortgage lender for assessment, and once approved, arrange-ments can be made for you to acquire the property. Either way, you can own the property and stay there, keeping up with the monthly mortgage payments if you have one, and live happily ever after.

Note that the information that I am endeavouring to convey to you today, however, is supposed to equip you with all the necessary tools to feel confident enough to not only get on the property ladder if you are not already a homeowner, but also to acquire your second, third, fourth, or fifth property … and so on. For reference, the average property price in London as of, October 31st 2017 was £400,000, so you only need three properties, each valued at this price to have a property portfolio worth over one million pounds. How fantastic does that sound to you?

By the time you have finished reading this book, you will have additional knowledge that will enable you to make a more informed decision to invest in properties and create your own portfolio if you so choose. As a real customer service enthusiast, I promise to be there for you at the beginning of this incredible journey. I am just an e-mail away and can be reached at:

timo@timorealestatesolutions.co.uk

should you need further advice, guidance, or support about any matter related to property investment or real estate in general.

Prior to diving into my book, it is a very good idea to think seriously about why you are reading it in the first place; what compels you to become involved in the world of property investment?

- Are you looking for financial freedom?
- Do you want the bragging rights that you own, say ten properties in London?
- Is status or prestige your ultimate goal?
- Are you seeking fulfilment in life?

Whatever you are looking for, I sincerely hope that the information contained in this book will empower you to achieve your goals. I am tempted to think that the action of buying this book alone implies that you genuinely want to make a big difference in your life. As far as I am concerned, you can. Trust that you'll live to tell the tale in 2-5 years' time when you've successfully made shrewd property investments.

The fact of the matter is that there is and always will be a significant demand for properties because people need accommodation or housing, whether here in London, in every other part of the UK, and in many other areas worldwide.

Every one of us needs a place to live regardless of financial status, age, race, religion, and location. This need relates to family, a student, a couple living together, a single person, a cabinet minister, a religious leader, a doctor, a librarian and even the Queen in her palace. We all need a place we call home, just as we need food and clothing.

The most interesting thing about property for me is that it is not merely a place to sleep in, but also a product or great opportunity to make a lot of money from. If you own your property either outright or have a mortgage on it, you will eventually accumulate a lot of equity in it over the long-term. If you decide to sell up, say in ten years' time, you will have so many options available to you for a brighter future. For instance, if you bought a property today at a price of £200,000 and you decided to sell it in ten years, it is very likely to have appreciated in value to about £500,000 or more, which means that you could easily walk away smiling to the bank with a net profit of at least £200,000. This figure accounts for the redemption of the mortgage and the payment of all the necessary taxes and related legal costs. I would indeed be so surprised if anyone could show me evidence of such a lump sum in their savings account from a single investment in the same period. Practically, it is quite difficult to save this kind of money even in 15 years' time, but with shrewd property investment, you certainly can make this kind of money, and more than once too!

It is for this reason that I encourage you to read the contents of this book not just for the sake of gleaning a tip or two, but to find something that empowers you to apply the knowledge obtained and go out and start making smart investments. If you start making them now, you will have that luxurious lifestyle you have always dreamed of within the next five years.

However, let us pause for a moment and conduct a simple reality check by reflecting on the following questions:

- Do you want to own your own residential 5-bedroom house with no mortgage at all?
- Do you want this house to have a swimming pool, a big garden, stables, garage, and a big driveway with parking spaces for at least ten cars, where your guests can park freely when they come by for dinner or your child's birthday party?
- Do you want to earn a passive income of £10,000 - £100,000 per month? Income that comes to your account whether you get out of bed or not?
- Have you ever considered sending your children to private schools or universities? Are you in a position to provide them with the proper education and environment to help them succeed when they grow up?
- Have you ever wondered why some people who do not seem to work as hard as you seem to have it all? ... the designer bags, clothes, two or more exotic holidays a year, the posh cars, to mention a few?

- Why them? Why not you? How come they have everything in life, and you don't?

Well, the good news is that you are in the right place, reading the right book and are on the right track to achieve your goals. As for the successful people you know, admire and probably aspire to be like, they may well be property investors or developers doing it part-time or full-time. Perhaps, they could be doing something else that has nothing to do with properties at all. Whatever they are doing, they must be very good at it, however. The fact is that they are successful, and they have that ideal lifestyle that you wish to emulate. I guess now comes the point where you are wondering why exactly you are not as successful as them.

On a positive note, this is not about them – it is all about you. You too can be just like them, and even be more successful. As previously mentioned, my primary goal for writing this book is to share with you the knowledge that I hold about the property and real estate business. I am hoping that you will be armed with all the relevant information needed to kick-start your investment venture, and when you go out there, you not only avoid many of the mistakes that some of us did when we were first starting but most importantly make those millions of pounds for you and your family.

Now I can hear you asking about those huge obstacles that are going to stop you from investing in properties. For instance,

- Where am I going to get all the money required to start buying one or more properties for my portfolio? I am just employed with no inheritance fund.
- What qualifications do I need to start this venture? I am not even a graduate, or I am, but my degree is in a different field unrelated to housing or investment. Hence, I have no experience in the real estate business.
- Whom can I go to, to seek advice, guidance, and support to make these investments? I wouldn't know how to approach the banks, real estate agents or conveyance solicitors to obtain a mortgage and then buy a house.
- How do I get a loan or mortgage to buy my first home? The mortgage business is too complicated with much jargon.

- Where can I buy my first property in order to have the best chance of making good profit margins? Given my income, the properties for sale that I see online are too expensive for me.
- How could I possibly afford any property based on my income and personal circumstances, including my adverse credit history? I already have personal loans and a student loan to pay let alone my high living costs.
- What type of property is the best for investment purposes? Is it a flat, terraced, detached, or townhouse, bungalow, or commercial property like a shop?
- How is the property market doing? I have read in the local newspaper that it is likely to crash soon. Perhaps this is not the right time for me to buy any property ... or is it?

Well, you need worry no longer about all these questions, as this book endeavours to take away all anxiety, giving you the necessary confidence, and most importantly the right knowledge to make the best-informed decisions about property investments. My objective is to provide you with the relevant information to get started, to show you how the property market operates and how to raise the necessary capital to start building your own property portfolio. Basically, I will show you how to run your business with or without any relevant experience or education, whom to go to for the best advice and guidance, where to buy the properties from, the type of properties that you need to buy for great yields, how to obtain the most suitable mortgage product to buy your first property, and the most crucial things, how to not only make so much money, but also how to protect your vast wealth now and in the future.

Once you have read this book, the end result should be that you have got all the essential information about property investment that applies anywhere regardless of your geographic location, as well as the necessary tools to get started. As far as I am concerned, every property that you see as you leave your house today and and on each street during your travels has great potential to make money for you.

Let us look at one scenario in which you see a 2-bedroom end-of-terrace to invest in. If you were to buy it at £250,000, obtain full planning permission to extend it to a 3-bedroom house which is then done by a professional builder whom you could pay when the house is sold, you could then resell it after three months once all the work is completed. Given the current economic climate and buoyant property market in the United Kingdom, it is likely that you could easily sell this house within just six months at about £400,000, making a minimum profit of £50,000 after paying the related taxes and all expenses incurred whilst converting and modernising the property.

To put all this into perspective, professionals do indeed earn £50,000 as their gross salary per year. Bearing in mind that today the UK national average salary is £26,500 per annum, then earning this amount of £50,000 from this one development project within six months is nothing short of incredible. If you decide to do two or more projects in a year, you can easily earn a decent income without partaking in the rat race where you earn less money and spend most of your life at work. It is all about working smart: working fewer hours but earning more money. You need to be in a situation in which your money begins to work harder for you, say a big lump sum on your bank savings account that pays a high daily interest so that you earn good monthly income without doing any of the donkey work!

The fact that you have taken the trouble to buy this book and are now reading it shows that you are keen to improve your life. I suppose you do indeed desire to be wealthy, happy, and healthy beyond imagination, and have total fulfilment in life. I invite you to please carry on reading.

Chapter 1: Laying the Foundations: *What is Property Investment?*

Property investment involves buying a house, flat, or commercial building for the sole purpose of generating a decent profit. You can either buy this property for a quick sale, hence a quick profit on a short-term basis, or you could buy it on a long-term basis with the intention of letting it out to tenants over a set period to obtain rental income as well as capital growth when it appreciates in value.

The rule of thumb is to buy a property which is sought after by many people at the outset and that you are confident will still be once refurbished. This then translates into a quicker sale or return on your investment. The trick here is to get the property at a lower price, as low as possible. The idea is to buy, renovate it to a good, modern standard, and then put it back on the market for a quick sale. It may be necessary to put in a brand new kitchen, bathroom, better lighting as well as new flooring including nice carpets so that it looks more fresh and attractive to potential buyers. As you can imagine, time is of the essence, as the quicker you sell this property, the quicker you get your money back in addition to any profits.

The ideal property for this purpose could again be an end of terrace 2-bedroom house, which with approved planning permission from the relevant planning authorities you could extend to a 3 or 4-bedroom house with loft conversion. As you may appreciate, this property does eventually become bigger so will certainly fetch more money for you compared to selling it as a 2-bedroom house, as initially marketed.

It is also advisable that you buy such a property in an area close to many amenities and schools. As a word of caution, please avoid buying large, expensive specialist properties because it is likely that there are going to be less potential buyers who can afford the high list price. This game is about broadening your target market, not narrowing it. The other factor to consider is that you may not have all the experience and knowledge required at the outset, especially if you are just starting out, to pull off such a big project with a lot of money involved.

Factually, the more potential buyers you have for your property before the sale, the better for you, as you stand a much better chance of selling it and recouping your money, as well as making a decent profit. Remember, this is neither an interior design project, nor will it be your permanent home. It is purely a business venture that must make you serious money at the end of the day. You just have to do what is necessary and regulation-compliant, then once your project is completed on budget and on time, you can walk away not only smiling all the way to the bank but also start thinking about your next project.

If you are thinking of buying a property for long-term capital growth, your best option is to let it out, thus enabling you to obtain the best rental income from the tenants who occupy it. In this instance, you may not necessarily be bothered about the sales price, because in the grand scheme of things, you are going to hang on to this property for a long period, say five, ten, or twenty years, meaning that it shall undoubtedly appreciate in value. The main beauty of investing in such property is that the tenants actually pay for your mortgage and you also receive disposable income whenever the rent is credited into your bank account.

Location

This is arguably the most important factor when making a decision to buy a property anywhere. As they say, "Location, location, location."

I personally think that this single issue is more significant than the type, condition, or even the price of the property you want to buy. It does not matter whether the property is of a contemporary, modern standard or is cheap and has much land available, the real deal is the location, and it is important that you get it right. Another reason why location is so important regarding property investment is that it is the main factor that people consider when looking to buy or rent. Bear in mind that whether it is a residential or commercial property, potential buyers tend to first look at their preferred location before considering the type of property. In most cases, they will prefer to pay more for a property that is properly located. It is therefore advisable to buy a property in the most desirable and profitable place available. These include areas that are most desirable, affordable, and sought after by ordinary buyers or tenants. This may include areas in proximity to train stations, for easy commuting to and from work, redevelopment or regeneration areas, big manufacturing plants or factories which provide employment to the local population, or good schools. In much of the country, there tend to be the so-called "hotspots" which are areas where for one reason or another, the properties there sell or are let within a few days of going to market. In these instances, there is healthy demand in that area, and as long as you buy a property in a strategic place there, you are guaranteed a quick and considerable profit. A case in mind is the huge demand from both domestic and international buyers for residential properties in Mayfair, and in the London Borough of Kensington and Chelsea.

Commercial property investments, on the other hand, also have much scope for re-development projects and potentially a higher return on the investment.

Case Study

There is a property that is located in Greater London with a lot of potential for development. This property which is an existing workshop with offices and stores totals approximately 650 m2 (7,000 sq. ft) and is situated in a mixed-use area with housing to the north and west and a small retail parade to the east. A petrol station exists on the other side of the road, which is otherwise surrounded by residential land use. The nearest station is about one mile with direct links to Central London; journey time is about 25 minutes, so the property is ideal for commuters who work in the City of London.

This property has potential for residential development subject to obtaining planning consent. A scheme for the demolition of the existing buildings and erection of a three-storey unit comprising eight 2-bedroom flats and four 1-bedroom flats together with a communal roof garden and parking in the rear has been drafted and discussed with the local London Borough, with written response to the same provided. A copy of the architect's drawings and response from the Local Planning Authority is also available.

Proposed accommodation:

- *Ground Floor - 4 x 1-bedroom flats plus communal areas*
- *First floor - 4 x 2-bedroom flats*
- *Second floor - 4 x 2-bedroom flats*
- *Roof garden*

With regards the sales price of £750,000 you would think that this is quite reasonable. As a property investor keen on making serious money, the onus is on you to negotiate a lower price. It all depends on your negotiation skills because if you are very good at getting a decent bargain; why not buy this commercial property at say £600,000?

I emphasise this because you will find your figures stack up better when it comes to selling the units on completion of the project, and you shall walk away from this venture with a healthy profit.

Let's look at the figures at today's prices.

- Gross income from the sale of the 8 x 2-bedroom flats (on the first and second floors) at the sales price of £220,000 for each flat = £1,760,000
- Gross income from the sale of the 4 x 1-bedroom flats (on the ground floor) at the selling price of £ 175,000 for each flat = £ 700,000
- Net income is therefore gross income (£1,760,000 + £ 00,000) less purchase price, less development costs and taxes = £2,460,000 - £600,000 - Approximately £1,000,000 = £ 860,000.

This is a great return on your money within 6 - 12 months.

As you can imagine, this could be a typical example of a great property development project in any part of the city where you live. Obviously, you are more likely to earn higher profits if this development site is located in a very desirable area. The bottom line is that there are numerous opportunities around where you live for you to make serious money in the real estate business, regardless whether you want to be involved in the residential or commercial sector.

Whilst looking for the right location to buy a property to let long-term or develop for quick investment return, please consider the following:

- Places of work – are there offices or industries in the vicinity which offer employment to the local people, including your new tenants or potential buyers of your property? It is a fact that such places are normally worth more.
- Accessibility – is the property you want to buy within easy reach of transport connections like buses, trains, motorways, or even airports? If so, this property could command a premium price for you now or in the future when you decide to sell up.
- Amenities – how easy is it for someone to commute to and from the local shops, supermarkets, post office, banking facilities, pharmacies, libraries, sports centres, health facilities, or parks? This could be even more important especially in a city, where many

people neither have nor want to own a car due to high maintenance costs.
- Education facilities – in societies where school league tables matter, this is an important factor, especially if you are planning to sell and rent to parents (or would-be parents). It is a well-known fact that properties within a certain proximity of very good schools can sell for thousands more. You, therefore, need to find out about the nearby schools and how good they are.
- Neighbours – there is no harm in taking a closer look at the properties in the proximity of the one that you are thinking of buying. By and large, people like to live near others in the same class, age range, or ethnic group as themselves, and so they shall usually be more than willing to spend more to live near the people they relate to.

So how and where do you find properties at bargain or much discounted prices?
- Auction Houses – this is probably the best source of buying a property at a reduced price. This is due to the fact many properties

at auctions are repossessions whereby the banks and building societies have to get rid of them as quickly as possible at a price sufficient to clear the outstanding mortgage, and often at a fraction of the property's market value. These lenders usually have insurance to cater to such instances, and because real estate is not the core of their business, their priority is to dispose of such properties as quickly as possible so they can resume their day-to-day banking business.

- In other instances, private property owners may want a quick sale for various reasons, for example divorce, retiring and moving from England to Spain to seek warmer weather, clearing big debts, or death in the family. It could be that their best option at the time may be to approach an auction house and have their property sold quickly. You, as a property investor, could also target such people who may be friends, work colleagues or relatives, prior to the sale of their house through auction. You may be surprised by the number of opportunities right there in front of you.

- Landlords could also sell part of or their entire property portfolio through an auction house for the sole purpose of raising money quickly to finance other lucrative projects. Either way, it is advisable for any property investor to make a trip to these auctions to initially test the waters and eventually find a great bargain to start your venture. There is no harm in approaching any landlord that you know may be in need of a cash infusion.

Tips for Making the Best Property Investment Choices:

- *Location, location, location – I just cannot emphasise enough the importance of this factor. Your decision regarding this matter alone will fundimentally determine the rate of success of your venture. Buy your property investment in an area that you are confident your prospective buyers or tenants would like to buy or rent.*
- *Type of Property – buy a property with potential to extend with an extra bedroom(s) or loft conversion. This means that you shall initially be buying a 3-bedroom property, but you will eventually sell as a*

3 or 4-bedroom house, hence fetching more money for you just through some strategic planning and creativity!

- *Play safe initially – please do not take on too much, especially for your first development project. I would encourage you to go for the kind of property that most people are in the market for, and as a result, are easier to sell, rent and turn a profit from. Avoid big projects that may require specialist and expensive tasks.*
- *Look out for opportunities for buying good properties at discounted prices from property clubs, newspaper articles, reliable estate agents, and most importantly, auctions. Conduct your due diligence and market research, and get started today!*

Chapter Two: Dream Big Dreams:
When and Why Invest in Properties

People always ask me:

"When is the best time to buy a property as a home or an investment?"

The simple answer is that there really is no ideal time to purchase your new home or that property investment. This is because it is relative to one's personal circumstances and preferences more than anything else. For instance, if you are buying a house as your new home for residential use, you are purchasing a habitation for you and your family where you can stay comfortably, as we all need somewhere to sleep. This scenario implies that when it is time for you to buy or move homes, it becomes necessary for you to do so at that particular moment. For whatever reason, you have no choice but to buy that property as your new home for you and your family.

On the other hand, if you are buying a property for investment purposes, say on a buy-to-let basis for rental income, capital growth, or both, then the timing of this purchase may be worth considering. Equally important are the facts and figures. For example, it is wise to determine the potential rental income both in the short and long-term if you are thinking of buying a property to let. You have got to ask yourself, do the numbers stack up for me now and in the future? If they do, and you end up making very good returns on your investment, then do go ahead and purchase that property now.

That being said, there is a multitude of other factors that may determine the value of properties both in the short and long-term. This obviously can influence your decision-making regarding timing to buy. It is always a good idea to consider all pertinent factors as you assess the viability of a property purchase. These may include:

- The state of the economy both at the local and national level. In a recession, for instance, property prices tend to be much lower, and so from an experienced property investor's perspective, this could be perfect timing as one can easily get great bargains of say up to 40% below the current market value during such buyers' markets. A case in point is the recent recession here in the UK from 2007 to 2012, when there were record numbers of repossessions or foreclosures every month.

- The efforts or decisions of the central bank, say the Bank of England, regarding interest rate movements. Basically, there is likely to be more property buying and selling if and when the central bank's base rate is very low. Due to policies set by this bank and the government, the base rate could be as low as possible, as it is now at 0.5% (as at 31st September 2014).
- The seasons of the year. It may not come as a surprise to you to learn that people tend to have different buying habits prior and during the Christmas season compared to the summer period. This, in turn, affects property prices because of supply and demand dynamics.

One essential tip or main priority for any aspiring property investor is to buy a property for investment at a time when properties are cheapest, say just a few days before Christmas, and sell at times of the year like summer when properties usually fetch more money. The latter is seemingly true when the sun comes out in the months from May to August, and most people are in a better mood to do business. At this time, buyers would be more inclined to do more viewings and make better offers to purchase properties. With regards to the quiet period of less activity, say October to February, there is usually a limited supply of properties due to the holiday season, and many vendors have other priorities.

Case Study

Mr Chris Williams was told by a friend that his old classmate made a very good fortune over the years from property investment. He then feels so inspired by his friend's rags-to-riches story.

Unfortunately, he has just lost his job of the last 17 years. Armed with his redundancy payment, he makes the tough decision to invest this money in a property, hoping to make a similar fortune.

Given the fact that property prices tend to be lower prior to the Christmas break here in the UK because of less activity in the market, he takes his time to find a property that requires modernising but is in a strategic location in a good neighbourhood. The list price is £400,000, but given the current condition of the property, he puts in an offer of £300,000 which is initially declined by the seller. However, since this party is desperate to sell up, probably due to the upcoming winter season which will provide little to no possibility of receiving a better offer, he finally and reluctantly agrees to sell the property to Mr Williams at the lower price of £310,000. With regards to the list price of £400,000, the buyer took advantage of this quiet period to have a new kitchen, bathroom, and central heating fitted, as well as a new lick of paint throughout the whole house.

As someone who has done his research and is, therefore, fully aware that his renovated property would fetch a higher price in spring or summer, he puts it back on the market in April, and when he completes the sale in early June for £430,000, literally walks away from the deal with a gross profit of £120,000, clearly illustrating the *advantage of buying and selling properties at the right time.*

Why you must invest in properties to achieve financial freedom.

As far as I'm concerned, a property is not simply a place for me to stay. As a matter of fact, I enjoy the comfort of my home, but in my opinion, my home is an asset that in a few years' time will enable me to make some money. For instance, I bought an apartment in November 2001 in East London for £85,000, but on completion of the sale in July 2007 made a decent profit on the sale for £145,000. This could, therefore, be achieved if one buys a property cheaply and then sells it a few weeks, months, or years later on to obtain the difference between the outstanding mortgage balance (if any) and the sales price.

In other instances, you could do what is referred to as "equity release," whereby you re-mortgage the property (without paying any taxes) and take out some of the equity from it for the purpose of doing a house extension, paying your child's university fees or wedding costs, and even use as a deposit for another property purchase.

- The biggest advantage of property investment is that you can lock into cheap money. There is a common myth that applying for a mortgage which I personally prefer to call a "loan," say £500,000 to buy a decent property in any London suburb, is a very complicated business. Believe it or not, obtaining a mortgage for residential purpose is a lot easier than borrowing an unsecured loan of just £25,000 from any bank in the UK. This is because most lenders are more comfortable with lending on property, which provides them with a physical asset as collateral. Provided that you have clean credit history as well as the basic requisites such as proof of identity, address, and income, you shall most likely be approved for a mortgage to buy any property of your choice within the means allowed for by your down payment. Now I ask you to demonstrate where else you could raise that sort of money to buy anything in this country. Perhaps you should try the local Mercedes dealer down the road and approach them for a loan of a similar figure to purchase five cars! I am curious to know the outcome of your conversation with them. Yet you would easily get this money or mortgage from most banks if you pass their lending criteria. So what is stopping you from using this money to buy a property, refurbish it nicely at minimal costs, and sell it for a good profit margin within the space of three-six months? Talk about using other people's money to make money for yourself.

- Property investment is not time-consuming if you have the right team behind you. This team may include reliable builders, agents, accountants, to mention a few. Following the case of Mr Chris Williams mentioned prior in this chapter, the idea is to employ a couple or so builders with proven refurbishment and renovation skills to modernise the property. This implies that you as an investor or property developer could even have a full-time job and do similar property projects on a part-time basis.
- Equally important is the fact that we as human beings all need somewhere to stay and sleep, a

place we want to call our home. It does not matter whether it is an igloo, hut, townhouse, cottage, mansion, or even a grand royal palace. For this reason, the demand for properties will always be present, especially in towns and cities where a lot of people from around the world are migrating to in search of employment and better opportunities. I do honestly feel that there are enough fish in the pond for everyone – the rich and well-connected people will continue doing their mega-billion deals in central London, but even for those at the bottom of the property development or investment ladder, there is always going to be a property opportunity available in your local community that could also make you a lot of money. I always see opportunities everywhere I go, say when I am driving to work or my daughter's school to drop her off and collect her. I could easily spot a 2-bedroom house that could do with an extension to convert into a 3 or 4-bedroom to sell a few months later at a higher price. Alternatively, another property along the same street could be turned into two apartments for sale individually or to be let out to tenants for a weekly or monthly income.

- Investing in properties could undoubtedly be one of the safest and most reliable types of investments you could make in comparison to stocks and shares, retail, or any other related business. It matters not whether your property investment is in London, Dubai, Hong Kong, Kampala, Beijing, Paris, Nairobi, Doha, or New York, it will never lose value in the long-term. It may rise in value quickly or appreciate in value slowly. One thing is certain, though – that your property will increase in value over a given period. All you need is a bit of good initiative, coupled with good management, and your property will allow you to pay for your mortgage instalments (if applicable), but also give you some disposable income as well as incredible capital gain over a given term.
- The whole process of property investment is relatively simple as you can start at any level and move up as you gain more experience and knowledge. You do not necessarily have to be very qualified or have any equipment to get

started. It does help if you have some deposit to put down for property purchase, as well as to cover related expenses such as valuation costs, solicitors' fees, and some money to pay for the bank's administration costs to arrange your mortgage (if required), but this should not be a hindrance because most lenders are more than willing to lend on property if you are eligible for their loans. Once you complete your first project on time and within the specified budget, you shall then have a proven track record that you can approach them with to move onto bigger, more rewarding projects.

- Regarding the economic climate in the country and how it could affect your property investment, rest assured that property prices usually keep pace with the cost of living increases and could be a perfect hedge against inflation. It is for this reason that many people nowadays prefer to invest in properties as opposed to pensions. Besides, consecutive governments in the UK do tend to offer attractive tax breaks to boost or maintain a healthy property market.

- Better yet, I would strongly encourage you to assemble a great team who will advise you accordingly about any aspect of your property investment venture(s). This may include the bank manager at your bank, as they have a vested interest in the mortgaged property that you acquired through them, the solicitors, estate agents, accountant, professional builders, and mentors to mention a few.

Having said that, each property investment or project requires someone to have the right vision, initiative, ambition, sheer determination, can-do attitude, and the right skills set to see it through from conception to the very end, and all within a certain timeframe and budget. Hopefully, the information in this chapter will empower you to do so and become a very wealthy person who will go on to tell your own story.

Chapter 3: Knowledge is Power: *Mortgages, Buy-to-Let, and Commercial Finance*

When it comes to buying properties, whether your main residence or a property for business purposes, you will need money to own that house, flat, or commercial unit to someday obtain rental income or do a renovation project for a quick resale.

There are basically two ways of raising finance to start any property investment venture:

- Using your own money say through savings obtained from an inheritance fund, redundancy pay or a gift from your parents. This is ideal because it costs you nothing as there is no interest to pay.
- The other option is to borrow money from a bank, a private lender, a property investment syndicate, a hedge fund, family members,

friends or any other lending organisations. Sometimes this is referred to as OPM ("other people's money").

1 would recommend the latter, and so I am going to spend more time dwelling on this option, just to give you more insight into the field as well as to provide you with all relevant information so that you can eventually make informed decisions about property investment. I am fully aware that many people, especially those who dislike debts for personal, cultural, or religious beliefs, may not approve of this, but in my view there is absolutely no harm in using a little of your own money and then using a lot of someone else's money, especially the high street banks who are in the business of lending money to people who want to improve their lives. Even if you are already rich and can afford it, it is probably better to adopt this attitude because regarding "checks and balances," you will, in turn, be more motivated to work harder to achieve your goals. If you are to invest a lot of your money into your new property investment venture, on the other hand, a natural tendency exists to

overspend the money when it is there because there is no outside control.

If you are to borrow money to do a property project, you are likely to be more motivated and will tend to be more accountable to whatever decisions or actions you may take. You will also be fully aware that failure to repay all the money borrowed for your business does have serious implications: for example, collapse of your business, and in some cases, even the loss of your own home and lifestyle.

The different methods that many investors use to borrow money to start their property investment business ventures include the following:

- Bank loans for business purposes - These are readily available, especially to those with a clean credit history and generally good track record. However, these loans, which could be either secured or unsecured, could sometimes have high set-up charges.
- Bank overdrafts, which are usually fast, short-term finance, but the disadvantage is that they may be "called in" by the lender at any time.

- Personal loans are unsecured, small amounts of loans (up to £15,000) and so quite easy to obtain. They are also acquired from the bank but are different from bank loans in the sense that they are meant for personal use purchases like cars or home appliances. However, some shrewd investors do use this form of financing to do small renovation projects to new property purchases for a big profit margin from a quick sale.
- Credit cards are also relatively easy to get, and once again, this money could be used as deposit for home purchases or refurbishment projects. However, these cards normally have high interest rates.
- Mortgages – with the fact that these are the most frequently used form of finance for most property investors in mind, I am going to dwell more on this subject. Hopefully, I can share with you some useful tips that will enable you to go out there, get your first property, and eventually build your own multi-million-pound portfolio. I believe that if you are armed with the right information from

this book, you can become a "property millionaire" within the next two to five years.

Mortgage

A mortgage is defined as an advance of money from a lender or bank to you for the sole purpose of purchasing a property, in which the property itself is held by the lender as security for the debt. It is only when you redeem or pay off the whole debt say in 25 years that this lender shall release the mortgage deeds to you.

The vast majority of people in the United Kingdom do buy their homes using the mortgage facility that is secured on them. The mortgage market has become increasingly complex over recent years with many different products from a variety of lenders.

There are a variety of mortgages on the whole market, and these include:

Flexible Mortgages

These are essentially repayment mortgages, but as their name suggests, do offer an added degree of flexibility. These are designed to enable the borrower to make additional payments when you have extra money, or reduce and even miss some monthly mortgage payments occasionally when you are not in a position to do so due to unforeseen circumstances.

These mortgages are very good for those who do not have a steady or consistent income, allowing them to pay more in a good month and less or nothing in a bad month. The borrower can also make lump-sum repayments to decrease the outstanding balance and considerably reduce the interest payable.

One of the most important benefits of flexible mortgages is that the interest is usually calculated on a daily basis rather than a monthly or annual one as with most other mortgages. Monthly or annual calculation means that there is a time lag before the amount you have paid is deducted from the sum owing, and hence before your interest payments are reduced. With daily calculation, the amount is credited there and then, meaning that every penny acts immediately to reduce the cost of borrowing.

By consistently making overpayments, one can save thousands of pounds on mortgage costs, and in some cases, be able to redeem the mortgage earlier, say in 15 years rather than the usual 25 years. I would personally recommend this mortgage product whether you have a stable income or not because in the long-term, you do save yourself a lot of money.

Another advantage of flexible mortgages is that the interest rate charged is often slightly lower than the same lender's standard variable rate. You can also adopt your own payment schedule in many cases say on a weekly or fortnightly, rather than monthly basis.

If you also consistently make extra repayments over a long duration, it is also possible for you to "draw down" further funds if you need them for any legal purpose, without having to re-mortgage or withdraw any overpayment you have made.

Equally important is the fact that these flexible mortgages do not usually have redemption penalties if you wish to redeem early. To a property investor who took out a mortgage on a run-down property that needs some renovation and then put it back on the market for a quick sale, this is like a gift from God in heaven.

The disadvantage of flexible mortgages, on the other hand, is that you may need a big chunk of deposit; say 25% or more to obtain them. They do not normally offer fixed or discounted rates, but the set-up charges could be higher than the standard mortgages.

Specialised Mortgages

The mortgage lenders tend to describe mortgage applications as "status" or "non-status."

A status mortgage is given to you if you meet all the lender's normal mortgage conditions which include having proof of identity and address for three years or longer, being employed full-time or self-employed with at least three years' audited books of accounts, and passing their affordability and property valuation checks. The majority of the mortgages approved and granted by lenders to many individuals for private home buying fall into this category.

A non-status mortgage, on the other hand, is one in which a mortgage applicant does not qualify for a status mortgage as he or she earns a good income on a regular basis but has no proof or evidence like pay slips to back it up, and worse still may even have an adverse credit history. One lender could still provide a mortgage to this type of applicant. Many of these mortgages are based upon self-certification, which implies that one simply needs to show that they can make the repayments. They have to truthfully declare that their income is of the level they state and are, therefore, not required to produce any payslips or accounts.

This may sound too good to be true, but it does happen. The main disadvantage of such non-status mortgages is that the interest rate may be higher compared to a status mortgage because the lender has to consider the extra risk involved in this lending scheme.

The other thing to consider is that even though it is always advisable to take out a status mortgage where possible, do not despair if the lenders refuse to approve your application for any reason. Failure to obtain it is certainly not the end of the world because you may be able to get a non-status mortgage to move onto the property ladder. Once you have saved enough money, make it your priority to eliminate any obstacles like your credit history, so that when it is clean enough again, you could obtain a status mortgage with a lower and better interest rate. It is also important to remember that one lender could only offer a more costly non-status mortgage because you do not qualify for any of their non-status mortgage products, but another may still accept you for their status mortgage. Hence, there is a need for you to shop around for the best mortgage.

Commercial Mortgages

As the name suggests, a commercial mortgage is for the purchase of a commercial property such as a shop, warehouse, blocks of apartments, care home, factory, hotel, private school, hostel, and even a portfolio of houses.

The main advantage of commercial mortgages is that there are fewer to no restrictions on what you can do with the property purchased. The mortgage amount available is also usually much larger in most cases.

The disadvantages of a commercial mortgage, on the other hand, are slightly higher interest rates, with the fixed or discounted rate deals unlikely to be offered.

Buy-To-Let Mortgages (BTLs)

These types of mortgages are specifically intended to finance the purchase of residential houses and flats for letting purposes rather than owner occupation.

The main advantages of a buy-to-let mortgage include the following:

- You can obtain one or more mortgages on different properties even if you already have a mortgage on your own family home.
- The rental income of the property is taken into consideration when calculating the maximum mortgage, and so your personal income is not necessarily relevant.
- Buy-to-let mortgages are relatively easy to obtain subject to a valuation and assessment of likely rental income. Some of these BTLs mortgage products do not even require proof of income.
- They are available for between 5 – 30 years and tend to be more flexible than a standard mortgage.
- Depending on your credit history and good relationship with your bank, you may sometimes even be able to borrow more money than the property is worth to finance the renovation projects on it.
- Buy-to-let mortgages may qualify for tax relief on the interest rate payments.

On the other hand, there are disadvantages of buy-to-let mortgages, which include the following:

- The interest rate is usually higher because from the lender's perspective you are more or less running a business in which you are receiving rental income from tenants occupying your property.
- You may need a larger deposit, say 25% or more to obtain the best buy-to-let mortgage deals.
- The irony is that having a buy-to-let mortgage may make it more difficult for you to obtain another mortgage on your own home if you need to raise money for any other purpose. Though conversely, having a mortgage already will not make it more difficult to acquire a buy-to-let mortgage.

Besides, buy-to-let mortgages are available with variable, fixed, capped, and discounted rates.

As a general guide, it is recommended that the rental income from a buy-to-let property should be least 130%-150% of the monthly mortgage payments if the rental project is to be viable and successful.

Equally important is the fact that if you obtain an ordinary or standard mortgage to buy a property and then decide to let it out, you must obtain the prior permission of the lender.

Second Mortgages (Secured Loans)

This situation arises when you buy a property at a certain price now and then find that a few years down the line it has appreciated in value and now has a lot of equity.

A case in mind is that of a client of mine who bought a good 2-bedroom apartment as her main residence in Notting Hill, London, at £85,000 in 1992, but as of August 31st 2014, it was worth about £900,000 with only a mortgage of £10,000. Hence she now has equity of £690,000 in her property. It is scenarios like these that make me so passionate about property and obtaining good return from doing shrewd investments.

It is, therefore, worth considering that the money which is tied up in your own home (if you have one) is a good source of business capital, especially if the house prices in London continue rising year in year out.

Now that you are familiar with the types of mortgages, I would also like to give you some information about the two methods of paying back the mortgage amount to the lender.

These include the following:

- **Repayment Method**

    This is an arrangement in which you repay the capital and interest in instalments until you have repaid the total sum. The payments you have to make every month are normally the same, subject only to the prevailing interest rate at the time. In the early years of a repayment mortgage, most of your payments go to paying off the interest and little or none of the capital. Only in the later years do you repay the capital.

This repayment method is suitable for property investors or entrepreneurs who are going to purchase properties that they intend to keep in the medium and long-term for rental income and capital growth.

- **Interest Only Method**

    This criterion of paying back the borrowed money, on the other hand, is one in which you only pay the interest on the capital sum you have borrowed each month, and also depends on the prevailing interest rate at the time.

    Actually, you do not repay any of the capital during the life of the mortgage but are required to repay in a single lump sum at the end of the mortgage period.

    The main disadvantage of the interest-only method of repaying the money borrowed, especially for private home buyers, is that they are left with a large capital sum to repay at the end of the term and in some cases may not have the means of redeeming this debt other than selling up.

This option could, however, be ideal for you, especially if you are a property investor or entrepreneur, because your monthly mortgage payments would be kept to a minimum yet your house or property portfolio could be appreciating in value and, therefore, be worth more than enough to repay the mortgage in full when the mortgage term ends. It is very useful for short-term lending as well as "buying a property for a quick sale" projects since you only make the payments for the interest and do not have to repay the capital initially until your project is complete.

Having said that, it is always advisable to combine this interest only method with a lump sum repayment vehicle like a pension, whole of life insurance policy, or savings that is designed to repay the capital sum when the mortgage period ends. You effectively make two payments – one to repay the interest and the other into an investment vehicle which on maturity, will meet the lump sum repayment due upon completion.

In terms of selecting the most suitable mortgage product, one of the most important factors to consider is the interest rate. There are many mortgage products on the market with a variety of rates that are designed to appeal and cater for different types of property buyers. These are mentioned below for your consideration:

- **Variable Rate**

    This is the standard arrangement for most mortgages. In the United Kingdom, for instance, most banks or lenders charge about 1.25% above the Bank of England base rate on their standard variable rate (SVR) mortgages. Hence, as the base rate changes, so will the interest you pay on your mortgage.

    This variable rate could be ideal for property investors since even though the interest rate varies from time to time, you will at least know what you will pay at the same rate relative to the base rate.

- **Fixed Rate**

    As the name suggests, with a fixed rate mortgage product the interest rate is fixed regardless of the prevailing base rate. However, this is only for a specified period in which you could choose 2, 3, 5 or 10 years, for example.

    The fixed rate is ideally suited to private homebuyers who are purchasing a property for the first time as this allows them to budget with some certainty.

    However, they are not always suitable for property investors because even though you will not pay more for your mortgage if the interest rate rises, you will be paying more than you need to if the interest rate falls.

    The other disadvantage of the fixed rate mortgage product is that they carry stiff penalties if you wish to redeem the mortgage. The only situation where this type of mortgage rate is suitable is when you are quite certain that you intend to retain ownership of the property in the medium or long-term; for example, you can have your mortgage with a 2-year fixed rate if you are expecting to live on the property for the next 2 years without moving.

- **Discounted Rate**

    The mortgages with a discounted rate usually have a guarantee that the rate you pay will always be less than the bank or lender's standard variable mortgage rate, for a specified period of say, two or three years.

    For instance, if the standard rate is 5%, a discount of 2% may be offered to you making your mortgage interest rate 3%. If the standard rate rises to 7%, you will still receive a discount of 2%, and so you will make the necessary payments at a discounted rate of 5%.

    A mortgage with a discounted rate may not really be ideal for a property investor because it only applies for a specified period. After this duration, it does not convert to the lender's standard rate that may not be competitive compared to other lenders' current rates. Worse still, penalties attached to mortgage products with these rates may make it difficult to transfer the mortgage to another provider.

- **Capped Rate**

    This is a combination of a variable rate and a fixed rate mortgage. The rate of interest you pay will vary, but only between an upper cap and a lower collar. Therefore, depending on the way interest rates move, you could pay more than the standard rate or less. The capped rate mortgages are primarily intended to make budgeting easier, especially for first-time buyers.

    In some cases, the mortgage with a capped rate could also be suitable for property investors who are operating on a very tight budget. Redemption penalties may apply, but these are often less onerous than for mortgages with fixed rates since the capped rate mortgage also offers the great benefit that one may choose to overpay as well as underpay, compared to the standard rate.

As an important tip, you should always do your homework and research before approaching any bank or lender to apply for a mortgage from them. This whole process may be time-consuming and at times very frustrating, but I can assure you that it will all be worthwhile in the long-term because you will save yourself a lot of money if you get it right. If the whole process becomes too daunting, there is no harm in approaching an experienced and knowledgeable mortgage broker who could do all the relevant research for you.

All this will cost you is your time and the broker's fees, but you will surely not regret this decision if the broker does his job well. If I can make another suggestion about this, please only go to a mortgage broker who has been highly recommended to you by a colleague, relative, or friend who has used him or her before.

Chapter 4: Seeing the Big Picture: *How to Invest in Properties*

There are endless opportunities when it comes to investing in properties both for short and long-term returns on your investment. As you may gather from the list below, the various methods of making money from property investments include the following:

- Buying a property at a very low price, say from an auction house and selling it on, (sometimes without doing anything to it) within a few weeks, months, or years later.
- Buying a property cheaply, renovating, and adding value to it; for example, adding an extension or doing a loft conversion for an extra bedroom and then eventually selling up for a quick and nice profit.
- Building a property portfolio and earning passive income through rent from your

tenants on a weekly, monthly, or annual basis. Basically, this is the long-term option that can indeed make you very wealthy.

More so, there are many other ways of making serious money from sometimes seemingly riskier, but more rewarding property investment projects.

A case in mind is land development, whereby you find a plot of land in your local area or anywhere else in the country which holds great potential for building your own brand new home. For illustration purposes, this particular plot of land could be a gold mine if you instead build a block of flats on it. It may not necessarily be easy to find such strategic plots for said development, but again, if you do your homework right, you could easily walk away from this development project with millions of pounds in your bank account. To put things into perspective, you could easily earn a decent net profit of £500,000 or more per annum if you do one good project per year, and I shall show you how in a case study later in this chapter.

Obviously, if you live in the United Kingdom, you must consider planning permission if you are thinking of developing your piece of land. The whole experience can sometimes be very daunting, especially to a novice property investor, developer, or entrepreneur, but who says that the best things in life come easily? In reality, if becoming very wealthy indeed was that easy, everyone would be a millionaire. The truth is that it takes a lot of vision, courage, determination, strategic planning, as well as an element of risk-taking to speculate about making the right choices when it comes to developing any plot of land. Having a well-executed development project is a very rewarding experience regarding monetary gain and job satisfaction. Regarding the latter, there is nothing as exciting as having an idea about something and then doing the necessary work to complete that project.

Considering property development, the trick is to identify and buy the most suitable plot of land, which when developed will undoubtedly enable you to make serious money. It is true that any land that is developed, say into blocks of apartments will make a decent return on the investment. But you shall earn even more money with more complex projects if you are prepared to invest additional time and money into them.

In my professional opinion, the land with the most potential for development includes the following:

- Sites in strategic locations, which means that they have access to good amenities, transport links, great housing in the neighbourhood, schools, shops, hospitals, to name a few. Basically, a good location will most certainly enable you to sell all the units that you have built at a relatively higher price, as there is likely to be more demand for them.
- Sites with conflicting use, a derelict factory in an area of new housing estates, for example. If you buy and obtain full planning permission to make a development of houses on such a site, this could be immensely rewarding. It could be a lengthy process, but again, if you are willing to push it through to the very end then you may be sitting on a gold mine.
- Sites that have a flat landscape are normally good for development. It is rare to find them,

as these are every property developer's dream, but if you find one, then grab it quickly as you will find that it is easier to build on them. Hence, you will spend less money on the building costs because you shall incur no expenses for levelling this land.

If you want to find the best plot of land, you could use the services of agencies or companies that specialise in sourcing such plots for property developers. Obviously, they shall charge you for their services, but it may be worthwhile considering they could possibly find the most suitable land for you based on your specific needs, preferences, and crucially, budget. They are usually well-connected people who know the areas they operate in very well and thus have exclusive knowledge about such plots of land even before they are put to market. Perhaps they were even born and brought up in that particular area and so are very familiar with the local market. If you can afford their fees, I would encourage you to employ them so you can benefit from their knowledge and experience.

Alternatively, you could do what most successful land developers do. Basically, they are on alert all the time. If they see a vacant or empty piece of land, that is any viable agricultural land or even a derelict building in the town, they will immediately approach the land or property owner to find out whether they wish to sell their property. The worst scenario is a resounding NO, but there is certainly no harm in trying. On the other hand, if by coincidence the vendor or owner of this land or derelict property was thinking of selling up and you approached them before anyone else had done so, you would then be in an excellent position to negotiate a lower price to purchase it. As you may appreciate, it is a numbers game. The lower the purchasing price and the higher the selling price from the developed units (for example: houses, flats or a combination of both), the more money you will make.

Case Study

The following scenario will help you understand how land development works and the potential for earning serious money.

Let us assume that you alone, or through a third party, have identified an ideal plot of land (1.5 acres) for development at the price of £600,000.

If you are a cash buyer, then you could purchase this land outright. However, if you do not have access to this kind of money, you can always go to your bank and obtain a loan, which is usually termed as a development loan or commercial finance. As long as you have a deposit of say 30%, you meet their lending criteria, and you provide them with all the relevant documents, you are likely to be approved for this loan.

Once you have bought this land, I would strongly advise you to seek advice from an architect or surveyor who will conduct due diligence and research on your behalf. Once this is done, he may inform you that you have sufficient space to build ten 3-bedroom houses.

The next course of action is to obtain a quotation from a reliable and reputable builder. In this instance, he or she may come back to you and say that they shall spend an average of about £75,000 for all materials and labour costs to build each house.

As a follow-up, you have to approach a local estate agent or property consultant who may advise you on the sales price of each house when it is finally built. For example, they may tell you that each house is likely to sell for £200,000.

Keeping all this in mind, you can then calculate the costs as follows:

- *The cost to buy the land and build the houses is £1,350,000 (£600,000 + £750,000, i.e., 10 houses x £75,000 cost for each house).*
- *The likely selling price of the 10 completed houses is £200,000 x 10 = £2,000,000.*
- *Therefore, the anticipated gross profit, excluding administration, planning, and finance costs as well as other miscellaneous expenses = £650,000.*

As you may gather from this case study, you are likely to make a gross profit of £650,000 from this project alone.

Besides, there is the other option of selling this land with only approved planning permission, for a decent profit as well.

Asset stripping

Another way of making serious money from investing in property is by purchasing other types of properties, such as larger farms or country estates, and converting some of the buildings into desirable residences – a technique known as *"ethical asset stripping."*

There are many experienced and successful property investors who have used this method to turn a property or estate that no one really wants into several units. Alternatively, they could purchase a property that is much larger or more expensive than they could otherwise afford. Basically, if the price is right, they could finance the whole deal by selling off carefully selected segments of this property, say a large farm, whereby land and a number of buildings, or one large building, could be subdivided.

Although you are buying more than you need, the intention should be to sell off the segments that are not required, or you do not want. It is very likely that you may need to stretch your finances initially to make the purchase at the outset, but careful buying and shrewd asset stripping could leave you with a fantastic country house or similar property at a knock-down price!

The practise of selling off land and buildings to recoup part of the cost of buying a large estate is common. However, when buying a large property, there are some important factors to consider:

- You need to be covered financially just in case the parts of the farm or estate you do not want take time to sell. In this instance, it may be a very good idea to still put those unwanted segments on the market while letting them out for residual income. After all, another investor may prefer to buy these properties when they are already occupied by tenants.
- You also need to seriously consider other issues like access, planning permission, and availability of utilities, to mention but a few.

There are actually some property search companies or knowledgeable individuals who specialise in bringing together buyers and sellers who want to purchase different parts of a single property. For instance, by bringing together someone who wants to purchase a property on a large farm, someone who wants to buy outbuildings for development, and someone who wants to rent agricultural land, a deal or compromise could be reached whereby all concerned parties benefit.

Claiming empty, vacant properties and land.

This may come as a surprise to you, but it is true that any derelict property or strategically located plot of land that you have seen for years or decades, down the street in your town, city or village could be up for grabs ... legally. All you need is some vision as well as a lot of research and some tireless effort. Basically, you have to contact all the relevant authorities at the local council, land registry, and local library to determine the ownership of this property.

This process could be very frustrating and challenging, and sometimes it could be that out of the ten properties that you start out to investigate, one or none could be the right one for a variety of reasons. The common one being that the son or daughter who inherited the property that you might be interested in has got "big plans" for it and, therefore, does not want to sell up right now, even though they may not even have the means or vision to do it. They could be merely have been dreaming about executing their big plans for the last twenty years! Having said that, there is certainly no harm in approaching them consistently to encourage them to sell this derelict property or empty land to you.

The enormous reward for all your tireless efforts over those months or years of trying to convince the property owner to sell to you means that you may end up buying this property at a lower price. Once it becomes yours, and you obtain full planning permission to convert or build some units, you will certainly be in a very good position. As it is a numbers game, you only have to refer to the case study in this chapter to work out how much money you could make from such a project.

Chapter 5: Making the Right Choices About the Ideal Type of Property to Buy: *Residential and Commercial Properties. Does Size Matter?*

Terraced house

This type of house is essentially part of a line of houses or situated in a long row of houses. These houses usually look the same and are pretty much identical structurally. Both sides of each house in the row share common rooms with a neighbouring house except for the houses at each end of the terrace.

- The main advantage of this type of property is that it is relatively cheaper than a semi-detached, or even a detached property, built or being sold in the same neighbourhood.
- The disadvantage of a terraced property, on the other hand, is that it usually has less

privacy, as two walls are shared, and sometimes there is a very small garden, or no yard at all, that comes with this type of house.

Bungalow

This is a house on one level with no stairs. If a bungalow has a room in the loft, it is then called a 'chalet bungalow.'

The word "bungalow" originates from the Indian word "bangla" which in the 19th century referred to houses built in a Bengali style. Bungalows were created when British colonial administrators adapted the classic Indian style low roofs and porches built around them.

They can either be detached or semi-detached.

- Advantage of a bungalow: the fact that it's all on one level. This makes it easier for an elderly or disabled person to live there, to install solar panels using the larger roof area with a right slant, to change room usage. For example, a dining room can become a

bedroom, and you can do more maintenance yourself such as clean gutters and windows, as everything is within easy reach.
- The disadvantages, on the other hand, include the fact that bedrooms do not get heat from rooms below. This type of property can also be easier to break into. It takes up more land as well; you may have a 3-bedroom bungalow instead of 2 two-bedroom terraced houses in the same lot.

Detached House

This type of house is not joined to any other property. It is a single standing property that doesn't share any walls with any other structure. Due to the isolation of the property, they are usually more private and generally more expensive than any other type of house.

- The main advantage of a detached house is that the free space surrounding the building is private to the owner and his family; depending on the local regulations and codes, you can do whatever permitted extension or

modification you would like and do not need to acquire a permit from a landlord to renovate or pay any property management fees like those paid by condominiums and some townhouse dwellers.
- The disadvantage is that all repairs and maintenance of this type of house such as any improvements including adding a swimming pool, large patio, or garden, is all at the expense of the owner.

Semi-Detached House

This particular house is joined to another house on one side. It is common to find a "Victorian semi-detached house" which was built a century ago when Queen Victoria was on the throne.

- The advantage of living in a semi-detached property is that there is still a level of privacy, even if one wall is shared by two houses.
- The disadvantages are that the upkeep of your side of the property still falls solely on you. Moreover, you cannot just plan extensive renovations and extensions as you have to

consider your twin house. In fact, it may be necessary for you to consult them before doing any works at all.

Flat or Apartment

A flat is a living area that is self-contained within a building. This type of property is usually situated in a building that is split up into multiple living areas for different residents.

The flat is part of a bigger building where all the other properties or flats for that matter, share a front door. These flats are normally found in very big towns and cities.

Advantages of buying and living in a flat or an apartment:

- One of the key advantages of an apartment is to provide security for your family in the event you are travelling, or being home to your expensive household goods.

- Facilities such as power and water backup and uninterrupted supply of cooking gas would help you to live a hassle-free life.
- An apartment which is part of a large development will have a well-maintained garden and landscaping as part of the complex to be used by the flat owners or tenants.
- Club facilities (in some apartment complexes) could provide you with access to a gym, sports facilities, and even a swimming pool which will help you to lead an active and healthy lifestyle – a must-have for today's high stress, fast-paced lifestyles.
- Services such as plumbers and electricians are usually available on call from the management company, which will help to reduce the hassle of maintaining your home.
- If you own an apartment and you get transferred with your job, some societies help the apartment owners to rent out the apartment, which enables you to generate revenue from the asset with limited efforts.
- No hassle with parking spaces, which has become a daily nuisance in the larger cities.

The parking slots are well-defined and allocated.
- If you are staying in a city where you don't have any friends or relatives nearby, it's always better to go for an apartment, as there is always the possibility that you can become acquainted with some of the other tenants.
- Availability of convenience stores within or near the apartment complex is very helpful as you can shop for basic essentials more easily.
- Apartment complexes usually have staff readily available to assist you with any matter, say collection of payments for usage of utilities such as electricity, water, internet or even garbage collection, which removes the hassle of setting reminders for such payments.

Disadvantages of buying and living in a flat:

- Maintenance of the common facilities comes at a significant cost
- Limited or no freedom to make modifications to the exteriors of your home
- Very limited space to develop interests such as gardening or owning pets

- Sound seepage between the wall of the adjoining apartments or voices from lower or higher floors could irritate you and vice-versa, especially if you have a nocturnal neighbour.
- If you are a believer in "good walls make good neighbours," then apartments may not be the best option for you. For instance, a particular problem may lead to a situation whereby you end up not getting along with your neighbours on the same floor.
- No flexibility to expand the space for future needs as your family grows, or if you want your parents to move in and live with you.

Other types of properties include the following:

Cottage

This is usually a small country dwelling.

Farmhouse

As the name suggests, this property is the main residence on a farm.

Converted barn

This is an old barn converted into a house or other residential use.

Mansion

A mansion is quite a large and usually luxurious detached house.

As regards commercial properties, they come in different shapes and sizes as you may gather below.

Overview

In the UK, The Town and Country Planning (Use Classes) Order 1987 came into force on June 01st 1987, replacing the previous 1972 and 1983 versions. It defines the possible uses of a site, with "site" meaning "the whole area of land within a single unit of occupation." The legislation is particularly relevant for those looking to buy, lease, rent, or otherwise occupy commercial property. The vast majority of property in England and Wales will have had its permissible uses already assigned by its local authority.

The Use Classes

The "classes" of potential uses are divided into groups. For example, the uses falling under Part A are types of professional service provided to the public and business communities, including the sale of goods or service in shops. Each part is further divided into subgroups, which each then contains the specific uses the law is actually concerned with. Each of the subgroups is assigned a letter from A to D and a number, creating, for example, a "Class A1 Use," a "Class B3 Use," etc.

Each class is used by the Local Planning Authority to allow them to create a suitable balance between residential areas and those for business purposes. They have the authority to effectively prohibit a "use" which would be inadvisable due to a particular property's location or other relevant considerations. The aim is to prevent types of business activities taking place which would have a detrimental effect on the local community. A hypothetical example might be to veto the location of a proposed heavy metal works, or a nightclub beside a school or housing estate.

The following information represents a brief summary of the property "classes" of use.

Not every use of building is assigned a class under this legislation. Examples include theatres, scrapyards, petrol stations, nightclubs, and casinos; these are known as *sui generis* uses.

Class A — Shops (including some services)

This heading is further subdivided into a variety of everyday commercial uses.

Class A1 — Shops and retail outlets

For those within Class A1, the customers in all cases should be "visiting members of the general public." Property in this area could include:

- Shops (where goods are sold)
- Post offices
- Premises where tickets are sold and travel agents
- Premises selling cold food (intended for consumption offsite)

- Hairdressers
- Florists
- Funeral directors
- Premises where goods for sale are displayed
- Premises where "domestic or personal" goods or services are hired from
- Premises where articles are deposited for washing, cleaning or repair

Class A2 — Professional services

Class A2 moves on to cover "financial and professional services." Again, these must be offered to the general public. This time, the specification is that "principally" the clients or customers of these types of businesses will again be visiting the premises:

- Financial services
- Professional services - except those involving health or medical services
- Any other services deemed "appropriate" for location within a shopping area

Class A3 — Food and drink

Class A3 consists of one use, namely premises which are to sell "food and drink" either to be consumed on site, or offsite in the case of hot food.

Class A4 — Drinking establishments

These include public houses, pubs, or wine bars.

Class A5 — Hot food and takeaway

This refers to the sale of hot food intended for consumption off the premises.

Class B — Further business and industrial activities

This class covers many common business activities and is prefaced by the provision for "all or any of" the activities described in Class B1:

Class B1 — Business

Offices - except those already mentioned within Class A2

- Premises for "research and development."
- Industrial processes which "can" take place within a residential area without damaging the "amenity of that area."

Since these classes are described in quite general terms, professional advice is advisable before proceeding with negotiations to occupy commercial premises. As the remaining Classes in Part B continues, the uses begin to relate to increasingly specific industrial processes.

Class B2

General industrial use; for example, carrying on an industrial process which does not fall within class B1 or within classes B3 to B7 below.

Class B3 — Special industrial group A

Relating to activities which must be registered according to the Alkali, etc. Works Regulation Act 1906. The exceptions are those activities which fall into the subsequent Classes B4 to B7, assigned to "Special Industrial Group B".

Class B4 - Special industrial group B

Class B4 relates to certain types of metal works, although not those carried out in a quarry or mine (or adjacent to one).

Class B5 - Special industrial group C

This addresses types of heavier industrial processes for minerals, again except where quarry or mine based. Some examples here are "producing rubber from scrap," "boiling or running linoleum gum," and "manufacturing acetylene from calcium carbide."

Class B6 - Special industrial group D

Activities can be broadly summarised as those involving work with oils, gums, resins, and some other types of chemical compounds, dealt with in Class B6. The first entry in this Class makes it clear that petroleum and petroleum products are not included.

Class B7 - Special industrial group E

Covers processes for materials of animal origin and includes 14 different uses. These range from process-ing potential foodstuffs such as the boiling or cleaning of tripe or curing fish to more general processes which nonetheless involve animal products. An example here is producing manure or activities processing "skins," such as leather.

Class B8 - Special industrial group F

This class applies to properties which are used "for storage or as a distribution centre."

Class C — Hotels, hostels and dwelling houses

Class C1

Use of a hotel, boarding, guest house or as a hostel, where in each case, no significant element of care is provided.

Class C2

Class C2 does cover such types of premises, providing they are residential:

- Hospitals and nursing homes.
- Schools, colleges or training centres.

Class C3

Class C3 addresses use as a "dwelling house" as a principal or secondary residence. The classifications were updated in 2010.

This class is formed of 3 parts:

C3 (a) those living together as a single household as defined by the Housing Act 2004; what could be construed as a family.

C3 (b): up to six people living together as a single household and receiving care, e.g., supported housing schemes such as those for people with learning disabilities or mental health problems.

C3 (c) allows for groups of people (up to six) living together as a single household. This allows for those groupings that do not fall within the C4 HMO definition, but which fell within the previous C3 use class, to be provided for, i.e. a small religious community may fall into this section as could a homeowner who is living with a lodger.

Class C4

Houses in multiple occupation - small shared houses occupied by between three and six unrelated individuals as their only or main residence, who share basic amenities such as a kitchen or bathroom.

Large houses in multiple occupation with more than six people sharing are unclassified by the Use Classes Order. In planning terms, they are described as being *sui generis*. In consequence, a planning application will be required for a change of use from a dwelling house to a large house in multiple occupation or from a Class C4 house in multiple occupation to a large house in multiple occupation where a material change of use is considered to have taken place.

Class D — Non-residential institutions

Class D1

Class D1 covers many "public" services which do not fall under Class A:

- Medical or health services premises which don't form a part of the practitioner's home
- Crèches, day nurseries, or day centres
- Premises for education
- Premises which display works of art without commercial transactions (sale or hire)
- Museums

- Public libraries or reading rooms
- Public or exhibition halls
- Premises "for, or in connection with, public worship or religious instruction"

Class D2

Class D2 addresses the use of premises for entertainment and leisure purposes:

- Cinemas
- Concert halls
- Bingo halls or casinos,
- Dance halls
- Swimming baths, skating rinks, gymnasiums or an "area for other indoor or outdoor sports or recreations, not involving motorised vehicles or firearms."

Sui generis

Sui Generis - certain uses do not fall within any use class and are considered *"sui generis."* Such uses include theatres, houses in multiple occupation, hostels providing no significant element of care, and scrapyards. Others include petrol stations and shops selling or displaying motor vehicles, retail warehouse clubs, nightclubs, launderettes, taxi businesses, amusement centres, and casinos.

Equally important to note are two types of property ownership which include the following:

- **Freehold** – the owner of the land, or freeholder, has total ownership of the property or land indefinitely. Having said that, they also bear full responsibility for maintenance and repairs of the property.
- **Leasehold** – a leaseholder has the ownership of the property for a period which has been granted by the freeholder. The date at which a lease expires is specified and can range from a few years to 999 years. However, the existing leases on properties are usually much shorter these days and mainly apply to flats or apartments.

Chapter 6: Sowing the Seeds and Reaping the Rewards: *How does one make shrewd property investments?*

Basically, the opportunities for creating real wealth in the property business are endless.

For instance, an investor could buy a property that needs modernising or renovating with the installation of a new kitchen, flooring, lighting, new bathroom, and a better garden which he does within a few months, and once completed, sells up straight away for a nice profit.

Buying properties over time with the objective of owning them for rental income or capital growth respectively is a clever way of building a profitable mixed residential and commercial property portfolio with houses, flats as well as shops.

Alternatively, another investor could decide to buy one or two ideal properties at a time, retain them for a while, and have a good return when they sell them in the future. This option could be a great income stream for any property investor or even turn out to be the best pension for your retirement.

Another strategy for making serious money from property investments is finding a property with a large parcel of land that has great potential for development. It is often the case that such an investment could provide other opportunities, such as the splitting up of this territory into small, independent projects.

To this effect, the possibilities could include:

- Subdividing this land into small plots, and when your application for building permission to develop them is approved, reselling them to a builder or developer for a good return, without you laying a single brick yourself.
- Alternatively, this land could just be re-sold as is with development potential at a much

higher value, or this property can be sold as a "ransom strip" to a property developer.
- The other option is to develop all the separate units yourself and then sell them on completion, again at a decent sales price to enable you to earn a great profit for all your hard work.

However, it is important to remember that good renovation projects of properties for immediate sale could be riskier compared to the long-term projects. For instance, if a project drags on unnecessarily longer than planned for, it means more monthly mortgage payments will be made and more money spent on labour, materials, and other related costs. Hence, the profit margin shall be reduced. To avoid such a scenario, it is crucial to make the right choices regarding buying the right property in the right location, that is, one that offers the best short-term gains rather than longer-term prospects. Regarding the latter, such properties include large ones that tend to have fewer buyers in the market for them – even though the price could be reasonable, the high running costs may scare off many would-be buyers. Specialised properties, for instance, thatched cottages and barn conversions, can also involve more risk, as it can sometimes be more difficult to assess their market value accurately which may affect the profit margin.

The ideal properties for buy-to-sell projects include:

- Those with potential for an extension or conversion. You may be surprised by the amount of money you could make by merely buying such a small property, obtaining planning permission for extra bedrooms or even another house if there is enough space, and then selling up.
- Repossessed properties that are usually sold at discounted prices, which could be due to foreclosure by a bank. This may be a great opportunity and especially so for a cash buyer, as one may not even need to do any work on the property and sell it immediately for a quick profit.
- Those in up and coming areas which are seemingly becoming more popular with buyers. This could be the result of new residential developments, industries,

infrastructure, amenities, and transport links which attract people.
- Small or cheap properties which tend to have the largest gains in value during periods of rising prices but slowest fall in value during periods of declining prices.
- Properties for sale that require modernisation or refurbishment work for one reason or another. They could make you a very nice profit if you buy cheaply and sell at a higher price, especially after adding extra value to it through remodels such as changing the kitchen, bathroom, and creating a better garden.
- Properties that are not mortgageable, perhaps due to structural problems, for which most buyers who rely on bank finance are unable to buy. If you are a cash buyer, these could be bought at a knock-down price for repair and resale.
- Properties with a lot of spare land – the main benefit being that you could strip down the land to have another building plot which could be immediately sold separately. Alternatively, you could seek planning

permission from the local authorities, and once you get the approval, could build a brand new house on this site, usually a very profitable option.
- In other instances, period and character properties could also be ideal investments as they tend to hold their value quite well. Moreover, they are also usually the first to appreciate in value when an area becomes fashionable. Hence, it pays to have that vision to buy at a discounted price when the property prices are relatively low and then sell up when they rise.

Top Tips for Buying Property for Sale

- *Avoid getting involved in a property chain because this could slow down your buy-to-sell process, which in turn could leave you vulnerable to fluctuations in the property market. It is all about timing and your approach.*
- *It is worth buying a property from an auction house, as there are often bargains to be had. More so, the completion period (up to 28 days) with auction purchases in the UK implies that you will know when you can take possession of the property*

you are buying, hence the big advantage of being able to plan ahead for the re-sale.
- *If affordable, be a cash buyer whenever possible. The benefit of this option is not only that you can buy a property at the lowest price, but you also save time and reduce costs as well as overheads.*

Once you have bought your property and completed all necessary renovations if any, before putting it back on the market, please also consider the following:

- *Plan ahead and pick the best time to market your property. During the beginning of the year and the summer months, there is more buying activity, and your property is more likely to be sold at an ideal price.*
- *It is also important to choose the most appropriate way of selling your property to cut costs and create a bigger profit margin. For instance, you could use professional real estate agents to sell more quickly for you. They may help in not only valuing the property and pitching the price more realistically but also in guiding you throughout the whole negotiation process so that you get the maximum selling price.*

- *Preparation and presentation of the property to potential buyers are also essential to fetch the best price and have the quickest sale. This may involve a new lick of paint, new decorations in the house, or garden maintenance, to mention a few suggestions.*

Making Money from Your Plot of Land

I guess you are wondering how on earth one could make money from a plot of land that has been idle for years. Perhaps you are thinking of close to where you live, or even your own property that has an extra acre or two of spare area which you do not and will not need. Personally, during my travels, I am always on the lookout for such empty spaces, and you may be surprised that countrywide there are many opportunities that you could tap into.

Basically, if you identify such vacant land and feel that you could develop it into a housing estate, an office, or industrial development, there is a good chance that you can do just that. Money is always the main question. Where will I get the necessary funds to build these units? Or perhaps you doubt that you have the necessary experience or contacts to make this dream a reality. I will cover many of these obstacles, excuses, or objections that could be stopping you from doing all of this in the next chapter.

In the meantime, you have done well to identify that plot of underused land. You may then want to find out more about the ownership of this plot and whether it has any planning permission. As you can imagine, if this land does not have this permission, it is worth very little, perhaps even as little as £5,000 per acre.

However, if this same plot of land had planning permission, it would undoubtedly be worth much more. It obviously depends on the location and your intentions for the development of this land. It is worth noting that any piece of land, especially in a strategic location and with approved planning permission for housing units, could be priceless.

Land planning and development, therefore, involves locating plots of cheap undeveloped land and, by following the appropriate planning procedures, transforming them into building plots which are worth much more after completion of housing units on them.

The fact that developed land can be worth much more than undeveloped or underdeveloped land is why land planning and development offers a chance of becoming a property millionaire even for a new or inexperienced property investor.

Obviously, this may sound easy or straightforward, but the reality is that if you are prepared to put in the hours and tireless effort, coupled with money and considerable skill from a reliable team of professionals, you could create your great opportunity of making some serious money from such projects. In fact, I find the most rewarding development projects are not so easy. Of course, you will need initiative, determination, and vision – and using the advice contained in this book, the sky's the limit!

How Can You Develop Land?

There are numerous ways you could develop any plot of land. As previously mentioned, just drive around your town, village, or city and watch out for any available opportunities. You may be pleasantly surprised by how many ways an underused piece of land could be put to better use, and more profitably.

Take a look at some examples:

- Residential Use – the plot could be used for building houses or flats. This is the most common type of property development. As you may be aware, there is a big demand for more housing units not only in the UK but in many towns and cities across the world, as there are severe shortages for accommodation for the growing population. Building rows of houses or blocks of flats in an estate and then selling them at the right time is likely to make you a sizeable amount.
- Commercial Use – shops, offices, factories, or warehouses. Once again, it is about looking at the bigger picture and carrying out the necessary research to find out if there is demand for any commercial units in a certain area. If for instance, there is no warehouse within a radius of about 10 miles from your

site, you may find yourself in a great position whereby you have the monopoly, and you can obtain a good rental income from your building; year in, year out.

- Mixed Use – this could be a combination of the uses mentioned above. For instance, you could have a building with six shops on the ground floor, four floors with 24 flats above these shops, a restaurant on top of this building as well as underground parking not only for your residents but also for the paying public. Provided you receive the permission for this development, this building could generate a lot of income for you on an annual basis through its many income streams.
- Other uses may include storage facilities, shopping malls, five-storey car parking buildings, sports and leisure facilities.

Factors That You Must Consider Whilst Choosing the Type of Development:

- Its location – for residential purposes, this land must be in a location where people can and want to live. If not, you may have to

consider the commercial option where you could consider building shops, offices, warehouses, and even a petrol station.
- The status within the relevant local development plan – although some developers have gone against local planning policy, it is not something that I would recommend. I find that it is much easier and sensible to fit in with this plan when possible. In the long run, it's advisable to refer to this policy before making an informed decision about the type of development you want for your plot of land.
- The cost of the development that you want on your site, as well as the likely returns. Essentially, it is vital to choose a development option that offers you the most profits. For this reason, I would always recommend having the right team around you to grant the best advice, guidance, and support so that you make the right calls. This team may include a planning consultant, an architect, a surveyor, builders, solicitors, or a bank manager, to mention a few.

Equally important is the fact that the most profitable and prudent procedure with land development is to agree to purchase the land *before* disclosing your plans to develop it. For your information, it is the actual granting of planning consent, and not the development itself, that substantially increases the value of the land. As a result, if you do not have a right of ownership to the land before the planning procedure commences, there is always the risk that someone else could seek to develop it.

This may come as a surprise to you, but some land developers actually carry out "blind developments," where they do not make an offer to the landowner about buying the land until later on in the planning process. There is a risk inherent to this option, as the landowner could decide to proceed with the development themselves, assuming they have the ability and money to do so.

There is also the possibility of setting up a partnership with the landowner if you cannot raise the finance to buy the land. In this instance, the way you approach him matters. In my opinion, it is best to prepare a comprehensive proposal to present and discuss with them in great detail in person. If it means giving them a few more days or weeks for them to seek legal counsel, so be it. Ultimately, if the deal is right for them, they will sign up, and you will both make good money from the project. Once you have successfully completed it, there is nothing to stop you from doing a similar thing with another plot elsewhere.

In this book so far, I have spent considerable time on this subject of land development, and the main reason for doing so is because this is where the big money lies. If you are seriously considering making large profits through shrewd property investment, this is absolutely the way to go.

Having said that, land development is not the only option for making decent profits from property investment. There are other opportunities, but the most important in my opinion is building a *profitable* property portfolio for both rental income and capital growth, both for the short and long term.

The top tips for building your portfolio from two up to one thousand properties here in the UK:

- *Do your own due diligence – please carry out the necessary research about the property market in the area that you want to invest in. If it is London, for instance, conduct a reality check first about why you want to invest in properties and not stocks and shares or high-rate saving accounts. Find out more about the type of properties you want to invest in, where to buy them, the so-called "hot-spots," as well as the available finance or buy-to-let mortgage products. In my opinion, it is better to invest in freehold houses. As long as you go into this with your eyes wide open and you acknowledge potential advantages and disadvantages, you will live to tell the tale.*
- *Do the maths and shop around for the best mortgage products – it is very important to be on top of your figures, especially with mortgage costs and rental income forecasts. There is no harm in seeking expertise from professional people like your accountant, letting agents, property consultants, or even your bank manager.*
- *Think about your 'ideal tenant' and the management issues involved. Do you want to be*

hands-on, or would you prefer to hand over your property to a letting agency that will charge you for the management fees?

You will make money from your property investments as long as you have done all the relevant research and are in the best position to run your portfolio successfully. As a gentle reminder, it is all about identifying what you want to achieve from your property projects, drawing up a master plan, and then executing it effectively within the specified budget and period.

Chapter 7: Where There's a Will, There's a Way: *Overcoming Obstacles to Making Money From Property Investment.*

As I have already stated several times in previous chapters, it is true that making shrewd property investments can be very rewarding. We all know friends, relatives, and property tycoons in our cities that have made money from real estate activities. The truth of the matter is that the property industry has been around for centuries and is here to stay as long as we are still alive. The beauty of this industry is that the dynamics are not changing rapidly as they are in other fields that have been irrevocably changed by the introduction of the Internet. In other words, one need not re-invent the wheel to become a millionaire or better yet, a property tycoon.

If you are still reluctant, ask yourself, what is stopping you from breaking away from your present position and making money through investing in properties?

I believe that anyone given the right tools and information could be well-armed to achieve their goal of becoming wealthy. If you have purchased this book and made it this far, then there must be a good reason. It might just be that you seek more knowledge about the subject of property investment, or your drive is the desire to achieve financial freedom. No one knows what the future holds, but you are starting on the right path to becoming well-informed to make the correct decisions for achieving the success you seek.

However, as you may appreciate by now, making money from real estate is neither rocket science nor straightforward. As far as I'm concerned, a property investment venture is just like any other business, which means it has to be run efficiently and professionally.

Regarding getting your property investment business off the ground, there are likely to be a number of obstacles which you need be aware of to take the necessary steps to mitigate them.

These challenges may include:

- Finance – raising funds, for your development project or building your property portfolio, now and in the future.
- The right knowledge and experience - having the relevant information at your fingertips to make informed decisions.
- Credit history – it does help to have a clean credit history to have easy access to funds from the bank, but even if you have adverse credit history, it is certainly not the end of the world.
- The state of the country's economy – this is true especially with the fluctuation of the interest rates set by the Central Bank, which in turn affect monthly mortgage payments for your home and each property in your portfolio.
- Personal attitude and work ethic - how risk-averse are you? What are your contingency plans if your tenants fail to keep up with their

payments? What about your team of builders who could abandon your project abruptly?

Each of these obstacles will be discussed further below, but I must stress the need to always have contingency plans in place.

Finance

If you are buying your first home or just building your property portfolio from scratch, the biggest obstacle is raising the necessary funds to be used as a deposit to obtain a mortgage.

Unless you have wealthy parents, have saved up over a number of years, or have won the lottery, it is very likely that you will have to apply for a mortgage from your bank to carry on with the purchase.

Given the current economic climate here in the UK and most other parts of the world after the worst recession in decades, many lenders or banks have seemingly become more rigid with their lending criteria. Hence, the requirement on their part to ask for heaven and earth before approving any mortgage applicant's case. It is not uncommon nowadays for the banks to request proof of address over longer periods, more details about one's employment history, and exhibit less tolerance to adverse credit history by requiring much larger deposits for house purchases, to mention but a few cases. This climate, therefore, proves it is quite difficult for any potential purchaser to receive a mortgage.

That said, there are numerous methods of raising the money needed for your projects. If anything, if people for various reasons are priced out of the market because of their inability to get a mortgage, it could be a blessing in disguise as there could be more properties around. This may in some cases create a buyers' market, and if you have some money to purchase your ideal property within a specific budget, you could find that you end up getting the same property at a very low price compared to periods of buoyant property markets.

Regarding raising the necessary finance, the details below are some of the options which may be available:

- Your savings, investments, inheritance, or even a gift from your parents could set you up nicely.
- You could also refinance other properties in your portfolio to raise money to buy another property. In fact, it always helps to review your mortgage interest rates because if you do so and switch lenders, you may find that you have more disposable income.
- Finance from investors who may be cash-rich and, therefore, willing to be passive by lending you money for a good return. These investors may choose to be directly involved in the day-to-day operations of your project, or they may just want to undertake a joint venture with you. Either way, you still get the necessary funds to kick-start your property business.
- Obtaining funds elsewhere by using your other skills. For instance, you could provide consultancy for property management, sales skills, or other additional task labour to help

raise enough money to get you started with your property venture.
- Re-investing any profits back in the property business. Once you have been working for long enough, and you have achieved your goal of hitting your sales targets, there is no harm in using some of this hard-earned money to buy another property to expand your property portfolio. Moreover, you could apply this strategy many times until you are completely happy, not only with the number of properties in your portfolio, but also with the returns you are receiving from it.

Knowledge

The phrase, "Knowledge is power" holds a wealth of meaning not only regarding property investment but also in all other spheres of business and life.

The beauty of investing in properties is that you need not have many academic qualifications or a lot of experience to start your venture. In comparison to other industries where a qualification is a must, all you need to kick-start your property business is a lot of common sense, the right industry-specific knowledge, and sheer determination to succeed. A good leader I used to know once said to me: "In many instances, you do not even need to have capital to start your business." He reckoned that "Your capital is your brain." This statement implies that if you identify what is needed to achieve what you want from investing in properties, you cannot fail to raise the necessary funds to make it happen. It may take you a few weeks or months, but even if it were to take you years, you would eventually get that money, start your project, and create the wealth you seek. For instance, you may want to build a property portfolio of 10 properties within 10 years, which is a very realistic goal.

The challenge may be that you do not have the money right now to kick-start this venture. My advice to you is to come up with ideas about *how* and *who* you could raise this money from for your first property. Forget about the 10 properties for now and just concentrate on finding the money or deposit required for your first property. I suggest that you write down everything as it comes to mind. You should be able to come up with possibilities like bank loans, credit cards, savings, gifts from your parents, soft loans from friends or relatives, fees or commissions to be earned from your on-going work projects, etc.

You may be pleasantly surprised that you could comfortably obtain these funds from one or two of these sources. The next challenge is to find the right way of approaching the suitable person, company, or firm to obtain this money. In such situations, it helps to do your homework right by drawing up a comprehensive property investment proposal, not only of how you intend to build and run your property portfolio of 10 houses for the next 10 years but also how you intend to repay the money that you have borrowed. By doing so, you shall come across as professional and organised, which shall increase your chances of receiving the necessary funds to get the ball rolling.

This highlights the need for you to acquire as much information as possible before and whilst engaging in this process. Hopefully, this book will be useful to you in this regard. In the meantime, I have compiled a list for reference (not exhaustive) of the usual jargon that is used in the property and mortgage industries. A glossary can be found at the back of this book.

Credit History

When it comes to borrowing money, especially from banks or building societies for residential or commercial purposes in the UK, most will use either Experian or Equifax to check your creditworthiness before making an offer of a loan or mortgage.

For this reason, it is vital to always be up to date with your credit history and ensure it stays clean. The simple reason for this suggestion is that the better your credit file is, the larger your chances of obtaining credit and the higher your chances of getting better lending terms with lower interest rates.

However, even if you do have adverse credit history for whatever reason, it is not the end of the world because there are also lenders who only specialise in the sub-prime market. The only difference is that their interest rates are normally higher.

Regarding the foreign property investors, on the other hand, this may not be applicable, as there are lenders out there who do lend their money specifically to clients from abroad. Timo Real Estate Solutions UK Ltd has all the contacts that you need not only to get the property you have your eyes on, but also to finance it at the best interest rates.

To find out more about your own credit history, you can refer to the following websites for your consideration:

- www.experian.co.uk
- www.equifax.co.uk

The State of the Country's Economy

Just like the subject mentioned above, the economic climate could also be a hindrance to someone who is keen on investing in properties. Unfortunately, this is a matter that in most cases is out of our control.

It is true that you could be managing your property portfolio well, but once there is a recession or depression that is not of your own doing, the impact on your business could prove fatal. This is because you may find that suddenly many of your tenants may be unable to pay the rent on time if at all due to unemployment. The other scenario could be that you are unable to re-mortgage one of your properties to carry out another development project, as the banks during these hard times tend to be more rigid with their lending.

Hence, the need to apply caution with your investments. For instance, it becomes necessary to have the relevant insurance policies to protect you, your family, and all your investments should the unexpected happen.

Personal Attitude and Work Ethic

Concerning making the most informed decisions and having the sheer determination to push through any property development project to completion, or building that property portfolio, it takes much hard work coupled with a positive, can-do attitude.

As this theory applies to all aspects of life, it is true what they say about reaping what you sow. I am convinced that with the right knowledge, contacts, and some capital, investing in properties is the next best thing since sliced bread.

For more motivation to help you not only get on the property ladder but to become seriously wealthy from property investment, I invite you to continue reading the next important chapters.

Chapter 8: Failure is Not an Option – Winner Takes All: *Property Investment Options and Solutions*

I have already mentioned that making serious money from properties is not rocket science. All it requires is good vision, initiative, and a proactive, can-do positive attitude towards any property investment opportunity.

Regarding raising the necessary funds to buy your first property as a home, or to begin building your property portfolio, the most common source of getting this money is through obtaining a mortgage from a bank or building society. In the United Kingdom, there are currently 125 mortgage lenders (as per The Council of Mortgage Lenders Directory, as at 25th October 2014), and so it may be quite difficult to choose the right lender for you, let alone the most suitable mortgage product based on your own circumstances and preferences.

Of course, you can just approach the Mortgage Adviser in your local bank or building society branch and apply for a mortgage to kick-start your property portfolio project. You may find that this is relatively easy because as long as you are eligible for that financial institution's lending criteria, your application will be approved, and you can buy the property. The main disadvantage with this option is that you may not necessarily get the best mortgage product compared to others from the greater mortgage market, as that particular lender will be selling their own products. This implies that you may end up paying higher monthly mortgage instalments unnecessarily.

On the other hand, it may be advisable to use the services of an independent mortgage broker or consultant whose job it is to be fully aware of the general mortgage market and, therefore, find you the best mortgage product based purely on your own needs and requirements. The main reason for this is that even though you may be well informed about financial matters, it is just too difficult to keep up to date with every lender and type of mortgage product on the market on any given day.

In my professional opinion, you should always go to a good mortgage broker who has been highly recommended by a relative or friend that has actually used his or her services. This is very important, as this mortgage broker will be positioned to find the most suitable mortgage deal from the entire mortgage market. In cases where you need a mortgage for a substantial sum or for an unusual property, this broker should be able to source and arrange a tailor-made mortgage for you rather than having a standard and maybe more expensive mortgage package deal.

Most independent mortgage brokers will charge you a fee, which I feel is a positive thing, as this is not only a sign of commitment from you that you are motivated but makes them work harder to obtain the best for you. On the other hand, the brokers who do not charge you a fee normally earn their commission from the lender whom they are getting the mortgage from for you. Hence, there could be a tendency on their part to be swayed towards the lender who offers the best commission, rather than the best mortgage deal for you.

Overall, it is worth doing your homework before choosing your lender or the mortgage/commercial finance broker who will be raising the necessary funds to buy your property. From my experience, this could make a significant difference regarding your monthly mortgage payments as well as your disposable income.

The factors to consider when determining your ideal mortgage product include:

1. Repayment Method: Do you prefer repayment, interest-only, or a mixture of both types?
2. The Mortgage Term: How long do you want it to be? In the UK, it's usually 25 years, but do you want to redeem this mortgage earlier, say within 10 – 15 years for less interest payment, or for a longer period of 30 years to make minimal monthly payments? The former can indeed be a great idea as you end up saving yourself a lot of money in the long term.
3. The Type of Interest Rate: These include fixed, discounted, variable, and capped to name a few. Equally important is the likely interest

rate once this fixed or discounted period expires. Do you prefer the peace of mind in the knowledge that you shall make similar monthly payments for the next 2 years, or are low payment instalments your number one priority?

Charges: You have to consider these charges that the lenders levy for setting up the mortgage for you. These may include valuation fees, Mortgage Indemnity Guarantee (MIG), or High Percentage Lending Fee (HPLF) if the mortgage is a high proportion of the valuation of the property you are buying. I would advise you to consider all the fees in total as well as other related costs like insurance, redemption penalties, and most importantly, the terms and conditions of the mortgage product.

There are three ways of raising money or a mortgage for any property project in the UK or anywhere else:

1. You can raise a mortgage on the property that you are purchasing for your project by putting down a deposit for it. This is usually the most common and easiest method.

2. You can raise a mortgage (or a second mortgage) on your own home. This is usually done by experienced property investors or entrepreneurs, especially when the property they are trying to buy is not mortgageable due to its poor condition.

3. You can still raise a mortgage on properties already in your own property portfolio to buy a new property or a couple more. This is the most ideal scenario because you do not have to use your own money to buy more properties. What you do instead is use the mortgageable properties to raise more money, usually at lower interest rates, to buy other properties.

The trick of the trade is to be ahead of the game such that you are in a great position to obtain the least risky and cheapest or most effective lending for your entire property portfolio or development project.

Set up a property investment vehicle or company so that you not only run your business in a professional and organised manner but are in a better position to raise money easily to finance your property development projects or build your property portfolio. The most common methods of doing this are trading as a Sole Trader, Partnership, or a Limited Company.

The main advantage of properly setting up your property business is that it becomes a lot easier and quicker for you to run. Moreover, you shall come across as reliable and more professional to all other business associates including the bank where you intend to borrow money to finance your property projects.

As a sole trader, you have full control over your business and a sole right to claim any and all profits generated. It's also beneficial for you to do this as it's easy and not as expensive to set up. However, the disadvantage is that you, as a sole trader, have full personal liability for your business. This could actually be a major hindrance especially when your property portfolio expands but has no legal protection from debts or claims. If there are any debts that have accrued, you will be exposed to unlimited liability.

With regards to setting up a partnership for your business, on the other hand, it can be positive to have some individuals working together with the sole objective of making decent profits. This is a situation in which up to 20 individuals may trade together as a partnership. You can, therefore, pool skills, time, and capital to do your property project. Each of the partners within the partnership is entitled to an equal say in the running of the business and profits. However, they each carry unlimited responsibility for any debts that are incurred in the course of the business. The most important aspect to consider here is that each partner is responsible for any debts which any partner incurs, even if they were unaware of them at the time. One way to avoid this or any other disputes is to set up a limited partnership and be absolutely clear about who is injecting what and who is responsible for what. In such scenarios, I would strongly recommend using a very reliable solicitor to draw up a "Deed of Partnership." Basically, it is a document that is not required by law but could come in very handy to avoid any future difficulties.

Finally, setting up a limited company, preferably a private limited liability company, which is a legal entity in its own right, could have a lot of advantages for your new property business. The main being that the liability of the owners or shareholders of this company for any losses the company might make are literally limited, normally to a nominal amount. Another advantage is that your limited company could be a good way of attracting other property investors into your business. In most small companies, the directors not only attend to the day-to-day running of the company but are also employees of the company. There are some property investors or developers who actually set up a number of limited companies, a practise known as a "beehive system" in which each investor owns part of the portfolio. The beauty of this arrangement is that it not only affords a greater degree of limited liability protection in the sense that if one company of their portfolio should fail, the others can continue unaffected, but it also allows different outside investors to be brought in on different projects. With a limited company, there may also be corporation tax advantages, especially when you first start your business since small companies pay less in corporation tax than a similarly sized sole trader business would. However, the disadvantages of establishing a limited company are the accounting responsibilities required by this type of business. Here in the UK, the accounts must be prepared by a qualified accountant every year and filed with Companies House. Secondly, because the company benefits from unlimited liability, you may need to personally guarantee any mortgages or other form of credit, which to some extent reduces the benefit of limited liability.

- Property Investment Syndicate (PIS) – This is an arrangement whereby some people who wish to invest in properties come together and pool resources as well as skills and talents with the ultimate goal of making good profit.

  The main advantage of setting up a property investment syndicate is that you can raise much more money and take on larger and more profitable projects from the outset, as opposed to doing it on your own or not even being able to do it at all in the first place. The members who join this syndicate may be either working, that is, they finance and actually work on your projects, or sleeping partners, meaning that they only put money into your projects. The disadvantage, on the other hand, is that you share control of the business and the profits with other people.

Key points to know about such property syndicates include:

1. Friends and relatives could make ideal investors in your syndicate. For instance, if your project requires an investment of £1,000,000, then you could approach 10 potential investors and spread the risk: an investment of £100,000 from each investor.

2. If you do not have suitable friends or relatives with such amounts of money to invest, you may contact your bank manager, any solicitors, or accountancy firms who usually know of private investors who may wish to put money into a property investment syndicate.

3. Alternatively, you may advertise for syndicate members in the local papers,

Internet, or real estate magazines and newspapers in their business opportunity section.

How a Property Investment Syndicate (PIS) Works

There is no formal legal structure for setting up a property investment syndicate. In fact, most syndicates operate according to a structure agreed upon by their members. In other cases, the members could ask a good solicitor to prepare a comprehensive, written agreement for all concerned.

Membership of a syndicate does not necessarily mean that the members own the property in question. This would normally be held in your name, or the name of the company. If the members of your syndicate wish to secure their investment with a legal stake in the property, it could be a good idea to form a limited liability company. Alternatively, you could form a legal co-operative, which is most suitable if syndicate members are actually going to be involved in the running of the property development operation or project.

Equally important is the fact that all members must be made fully aware of what is involved. Hence, they should know that there is a possibility of making a decent profit or even lose money on a project for various reasons.

As regards the number of members in a syndicate, there is no minimum or maximum size. It all depends on a number of factors like the duration of the project, level of investment, and anticipated returns to name a few. That being said, a syndicate between 5 and 20 members is ideal. Regarding the shares, this should be done by allocating each member a share in proportion to each member's cash incentive into the syndicate.

Once each member has paid over the cash to you, you can proceed with your property projects. It is advisable to always keep all the members in your syndicate well informed about any progress or development, including the properties you have purchased, the renovation tasks, and costs, etc. This must also be done whenever each project is completed and at the end of each year during which the prepared accounts indicating all the expenses incurred, the total income received, and the net profit generated. It is this profit that is then distributed accordingly, based on the investment of each member.

In conclusion, setting up a syndicate is a great way of getting started in the property industry, especially if you have little or no money to make any investment. Basically, the strategy is for you to work hard, get your property project off the ground, manage it professionally, and complete it in the specified period allocated for maximum return.

Once you achieve this objective, you can use your own profits from this particular syndicate to set up a bigger and more profitable one in which you invest money into the new development project, eventually increasing your profits each time. If you consistently follow this business model over a few years, you could find yourself in a position in which you no longer need investors, as you will have accrued enough assets to take on any project on your own – then all the profits become yours!

In the next chapter, you will find a list of real-life examples of self-made property millionaires who, despite the odds, have managed to achieve their goal of having financial freedom and are now enjoying a dream lifestyle.

Chapter 9: He Who Dares, Wins: *My Personal Journey and Thoughts*

When I began writing the concluding chapter of this book, I saw a lot of flashing images, thoughts, and ideas, all going through my mind. Many questions were raised:

- Why did I decide to write this business book in the first place?
- Once published, who will be the most suitable reader for it?
- Who is really interested in property investment, and do they see the huge rewards it may bring?
- Who are those people who dare to dream?
- I have never written a book before, so how come I am doing the last chapter now after all those years of dreaming about doing this and the last six months or so, writing it?

- What is the ultimate message that I wish to convey to you, the reader, who has parted with your hard-earned money to not only buy this book but also spare valuable time reading it?

This book may perhaps be the product of the soul-searching that I have gone through especially in the last three years, to find out more about myself as well as the people in my local community. I now live in a wonderful country (Great Britain) that took me in whole-heartedly. On the other hand, it is also due to those other insecurities that we all have at one time or another.

During this chapter, I will answer most of the questions mentioned above and share with you some of my personal thoughts and theories on the journey from "the university of life." I hope you can draw some comparisons to your own life and gain inspiration from these few thoughts, finding the increased motivation to go on and achieve all your goals in life.

When I started out in the property business, I was making some good money, and I was living quite comfortably, but at one point, I lost pretty much everything. I was then back to square one. This is why I wanted to share all this knowledge with you, as there is nothing quite like doing something incorrectly the first time to make sure you do it right next time.

So, here I am running and managing my own property company and also writing this book. I intend to achieve my ambitious personal goals of absolute financial freedom within five years' time. My dream is to retire and carry out all the charity work I have longed to do, with the knowledge that I don't even have to get out of bed to earn my living.

The main reasons for me writing this book:

1. Kirsty Muwanguzi - my daughter, who is now 10 years old. She is the main reason why I decided to get out of my comfort zone and do something that I have never done before: writing a book! I do believe that as her proud dad, I must be the best role model I can ever be to her. I really want to have a

legacy that she can be so proud of. When she grows up and learns about how her migrant parents, her mum Olivia and I, moved to the UK from Uganda and sacrificed a lot for her in order for her to have a better upbringing than we did, she will also be inspired to achieve greater things in her life. Hopefully, we shall be a real testament that despite any odds or obstacles, such as a poor upbringing, prejudice, and little or no education, that anyone can succeed in anything they want to achieve.

I suppose it's also my way of thanking her for being there for me when I was really down. I vividly remember when my phone never used to ring because no one had any time for me because I had lost everything. Little did they know that it was me taking some time out to reflect on things. I was back to the drawing board, doing research for my new business venture, and at the same time, thinking of writing this book. As they say, most people will almost certainly be drawn to you if they think that they can get something from you. The reverse is true as well, as without a dime to your name, most people would not bother about you. Rightly or wrongly, I felt like I had been abandoned, and I was living more or less a reclusive lifestyle, but the one person who never deserted me was my daughter, who even at such a tender age gave me the biggest cuddles and innocent smiles that just kept me going! Up to this day, I cannot figure how she would work out that I was sad or lost in thoughts ... She would come to me and ask, "Why are you sad, Daddy?" then would hug me or smile and all the worries or anxieties would melt away. Obviously, not for good but at least for that moment, I would have no worries in the world. And for that, I will always be so grateful to her.

She has always wanted to be part of this book project as she keeps on asking me what the book is all about. When she wakes up tomorrow morning, I am going to ask her to write whatever she knows about houses and why Dad is so passionate about them. The reason for my writing this book is not only personal self-development but also to enable others not only to know more about the real estate industry but to avoid the early mistakes I made, and, most importantly to raise awareness that anyone can make serious money from investing in properties if you have the right knowledge. Many people believe that buying a property and obtaining a mortgage from a lender is a very complicated business. I have actually been to many gatherings, meetings, and parties where people have asked me what I do for a living, and when I tell them that I am a real estate person or mortgage consultant, I get bombarded with the most basic of questions: What is a mortgage? What about buy-to-lets? Hopefully, the simple diction and tone used in this book as well as the glossary of the terms will make it easier for anyone to become fully aware of the basics of this industry.

2. Equally important is the fact that there is the real possibility for you to make much money from properties. The source of income could be through renting your portfolio for passive income on a weekly, monthly, or annual basis;

re-mortgaging to release equity from your property; property sales for a quick sale (short-term) or capital growth (long-term); asset stripping; property development – all of which have been covered in this book.

Whatever you decide to do to your property or portfolio, you may eventually find that it is actually more or less like a milking a cow: whenever you need milk, you can just get it from your cow. Similarly, whenever the need for money arises for any purpose, say to buy a new car, that special round-the-world trip, wedding, debt consolidation, you name it, you can rest assured you can raise money from your property. I believe that some of the topics covered in this book will not only provide you with the relevant information and the necessary tools but also provide you with the inspiration to get your property business empire, or portfolio, off the ground right now. As one book that I read a while ago states, you may feel the fear to do this but do it anyway. At the end of this chapter, I will give you some real-life examples of self-made people who have made it, from rags to riches, purely through property investment.

Besides, there is the small matter of who is going to buy this book (my 2nd question). Well, if you have found the content of this book informative and helpful, why not spread the word so that all your friends, relatives, workmates or business associates, get a hard copy or get it on Kindle through Amazon. Perhaps, you could buy it for them as a present. On a serious note, as they say, "Knowledge is power". Hence, the need to empower ourselves with the right information so that we also achieve the financial freedom and the various options it brings to our lives. If all those property investors whom you know can achieve all that success through shrewd property investments, why not you? Are the so-called property tycoons that we always hear about in the newspapers or on the Internet any different from you or me? Certainly not!

If you are tired of the rat race, always trying to make ends meet at the end of every month when you get your salary, not had a nice holiday or vacation for more than 12 months, cannot give up work because of your monthly financial commitments such as your rent or mortgage instalments on your own home, car hire purchase, credit card or other bank loans, the information in this book is definitely for you. This content is also intended for you if you are dreaming of that better lifestyle; whatever that might look like to you ... rest assured you are now armed with some good knowledge to start your property portfolio.

With reference to one of the questions above, I do care about making the right property investments because this is how you become wealthy. I honestly believe that we all deserve a break in life, as well as a good taste for the finer things. I remember someone telling me a few years ago that they would rather die young than live long whilst poor, or even die young than being so old and poor! To me, this does not make much sense, but I do get the logic behind it in the sense that, being very poor can make you very vulnerable. It's like you have no options, and your life-choices are limited. The good news is that life does not need to be this grim, especially when we are empowered by such knowledge that is within this book that could create a turning point for many.

I can even remember the time and day when I first came to England. It's 20 years ago now, and boy it's been a tough ride indeed! My mama used to say that, "Miracles do happen," and for me, it's true. There have been many instances in my life whereby I have faced some real challenges, but somehow either by the workings of this universe, destiny, or the Grace of God, I have been able to overcome these obstacles or problems. For me as a Christian, I think it's the latter because of my faith – for you, the reasons you overcome your challenges may resonate differently.

Unfortunately, we cannot just rely on these perceived solutions to achieve our goals – we have to make them happen. Here are some of my thoughts and theories on the important skills and mindset needed to have a successful life:

- Good listening is a great skill. I am personally very fond of talking to anyone and everyone simply because you never know how and what that little chat could lead to. It does not matter whom you are talking to as I honestly feel that we are all indispensable in our own unique ways that we can always learn from each other. Besides, I also take some time to have a good think in isolation – fantastic if you have never tried it!

- Identifying who you are and what you want to achieve in life is a big one. I do believe that once you figure out your strengths and weaknesses, as well as what you want to achieve out of your life, you will create a sense of direction and purpose to succeed in all your endeavours.
- Making the right choices about your lifestyle, friends you hang out with, career, partner (be it love or business), and critical thinking or decision-making about your future. There is absolutely no point in hanging around negative people who are not going to encourage you to go for your dreams. If necessary, drop them as soon as you can, because sometimes, it's this ruthless streak that will carry you through those difficult or challenging times.
- My good friend, Clare TM has put a message today on Facebook along the lines, "Your smile is your logo, your personality is your business card." I do love this statement

because it holds a lot of meaning. The emphasis here is "personality," for the simple reason being that for you to relate to people of all walks of life and achieve whatever you need them to do for you or to work with you, you need to have the right personality and attitude both in body and spirit.
- Equally important are the two facts: it's not just what you know, it's also who you know. If and when you do get this balance right, you will certainly go places.

Regarding property investments, these traits will come in very handy as you approach and deal with real estate agents, who may pass over discounted properties to you for modernisation and a quick sale, solicitors who connect with you and go out of their way to process your case faster, and more importantly, to avoid the deal falling through. If you also have all the right knowledge about the most suitable mortgage product for your investment, which in turn helps you earn more disposable income from your rental payments by your tenant, you will certainly do well. People always talk about having so much capital to build their property portfolio, but as you gather, there is more to it than just money; these simple things are also vital, as they pay a crucial role in the day-to-day building and running of your property portfolio or development project.

The message that I want to convey to you my dear reader is that this is your time to become wealthy and successful. I have shown you how; you can choose an idea or two from the content of this book and then start your amazing journey. Think about this for a second; if an immigrant like me from Uganda to England can do it, why not you, who was actually born and brought up in this country, which is perhaps the best country in the world with its many opportunities? It is true that you know the system well, but you now have access to this book, the Internet, as well as all the other information from the many libraries around you, along with family support to give you the kick-start. So tell me ... what is stopping you from making money investing in property? Take it from me – you are in an excellent and blessed position to do something great in life.

Always remember that:

"Where there's a will, there's a way."

If you really want to be successful in life and lead the lifestyle you want, you will certainly go out and do this now. I am just a phone call, text, or e-mail away and always eager to hear about your success story.

All the successful property investors mentioned below followed exactly what you are about to embark on, and look at where they are now. I am pretty certain that when they started out, they had many reservations and concerns, but they took the risk, persevered, and made it!

Mr. Kevin Green, one of Britain's biggest landlords with an estimated fortune of £29m.

This entrepreneur from Carmarthenshire, Wales was a dyslexic boy who struggled at school, lived on the streets for a while, and then eventually became a multi-millionaire.

The story is often told of how he went from living on the streets as a teenager following a row over the family farm, to setting up his own property empire.

Apparently, he always knew that he wanted to be a millionaire, but his dream seemed far from reality when he found himself homeless at the age of 19.

The property developer, now aged 50, has a long story to tell, but he bought his first house on a buy-to-let mortgage, using credit cards for the deposit and a loan from his aunt. "I was very nervous when I signed the mortgage," he said, "it was one of the most nerve-wracking things I had ever done."

However, the risk paid off as after doing the house up, he sold it on for a profit of £8,100. This led to him buying another property, which again he sold for a profit.

Now Kevin is a multi-millionaire who owns more than 700 properties and is one of the UK's largest property landlords.

He recalled that for two years, he wasn't interested in anything but becoming a millionaire. He knew he had to be successful. He knew that it could happen if he worked hard enough. He would target houses he could add value to, which had a very strong rental market and were also easy to sell.

Kevin's advice to other budding property investors or entrepreneurs is that you've got to follow your heart and you've got to be passionate about what you do.

He says the reason for his success is that he is a determined, independent, pedantic individual. The difference between normal people and entrepreneurs is that they have got to make things happen. It's better to try and fail than not to try at all.

Mrs. Zhang Xin: The Chinese real estate developer who is worth $3.6 billion.

This is a typical example of a self-made female property billionaire from Beijing, China.

The story goes that she grew up in abject poverty brought up by a single mother, enduring much hardship, and at the age of 14 began a labouring project in a factory. Zhang, 47 years old, was born in Beijing just before Mao Zedong's Cultural Revolution when educated people like her parents were sent to the fields for "re-education." She says that she was born and grew up when the city was very quiet: no cars, no shops, no lights, no machines. People were just on bicycles.

At 14, she and her mother moved to Hong Kong where she spent five years in low-paid factory jobs, manufacturing toys, clothes, and electronics, trying to save enough to come to England to seek a decent education.

As an immigrant in Hong Kong, with no education, no background, she didn't even speak the local language or dialect, Cantonese, and it was just a hard way to live in Hong Kong, she recalled.

It took Zhang five years to save enough money for a plane ticket to London to study an English language course. She eventually won a scholarship to university, studied for a master's degree in economics at Cambridge University and landed her first job at Goldman Sachs in New York.

Instead of remaining in her comfortable life on Wall Street, Zhang returned to Beijing, where she met her husband Pan Shiyi, and together they started SOHO China in 1995, Since then, this company has become China's largest commercial real estate developer with 56 million square feet in prime developments in Beijing and Shanghai.

Not only does Zhang's rags-to-riches story mirror that of China itself, but it is Zhang who has shaped much of the country's modern urban landscape, with the logo of her company SOHO China on the side of buildings wherever you turn in Beijing.

SOHO China has 18 developments in Beijing, many of them landmark buildings, and has also expanded into Shanghai where it has bought or built 11 properties.

Apart from my great admiration for how she has managed to build and manage such a big, successful property business, I am also very impressed by her attitude towards the trappings of wealth, with her even suggesting her 14-year-old son find a job in McDonald's or KFC. Unfortunately, his application for the job was turned down due to his age, but again it just shows you this woman's humility. In my opinion, she is really an amazing and great role model.

As you can imagine, there are many other successful property entrepreneurs, investors, or developers here in the UK and around the world, bold men and women, who despite the odds have built their property empires from scratch. Bearing in mind the examples mentioned above of Kevin and Zhang, you too could live to tell your own story starting from scratch today, right here, right now!

So regardless of your current personal circumstances, status, academic qualifications, lack of knowledge, inexperience, or any other obstacle that you can think of, what are you waiting for to take the necessary steps now to become wealthy, achieve financial freedom, fulfilment in life, and create your own legacy?

A Glossary of Property Terms

Mortgage
A loan that is secured against a property.

Mortgagor
The mortgage borrower.

Mortgagee
The mortgage lender, usually a bank or building society.

Balance outstanding
The amount of money or loan owed to the lender at a particular time.

Bank
A lending institution for mortgages.

Building society
A mutual institution owned by its investors and borrowers that provides a range of savings and mortgage lending products; for example, the Nationwide Building Society.

Flexible mortgage
An arrangement enabling the mortgage borrower to increase and decrease payments as they wish (within certain limits).

Discounted rate mortgage
A discount offered by mortgage lenders to new borrowers, reducing monthly mortgage costs often during the first two or three years of the loan period.

Capped rate mortgage
A mortgage repayment scheme in which there is a fixed upper limit, or cap, to the interest payable, but where the standard variable interest rate applies when it is lower than the capped rate.

Repayment mortgage
A mortgage that accumulates monthly interest combined with payment towards the original sum borrowed.

Joint mortgage
A mortgage shared jointly between two people with the agreement that if one dies the other automatically inherits the other share.

Buildings insurance
Insurance against the cost of rebuilding a property from scratch following structural damage; for example, from fire, flood or storm.

Contents insurance
Insurance against accidental damage or theft of all moveable contents, including furniture, appliances, and soft furnishings.

Building regulations
The health and safety requirements that any new building or significant redevelopment must meet.

Exchange of contracts
The time when the buying and selling of a property becomes legally binding.

Completion
The point at which all financial transactions are complete, and the purchaser becomes the legal owner of a property.

Auction
The sale of a property to the highest bidder.

Annual Percentage Rate
The total cost of a loan, including all interest charges and arrangement fees, shown as a percentage rate and easily comparable with mortgage interest rates.

Cash back mortgage
A cash refund incentive offered by mortgage lenders to attract new borrowers, calculated as a small percentage of the mortgage advance.

Conveyancing
The legal process involved in buying and selling property or land.

Conveyancer
Legally trained individual who conducts the conveyance.

Covenant
An undertaking to do or not to do a certain course of action.

Deposit
The sum of money that the buyer puts down to secure the mortgage loan after the exchange of contracts; 10% of the purchase price, for example.

Early Redemption
The completion of mortgage repayments before the agreed upon term.

Equity
The difference between the value of a property and the amount f mortgage owed on it.

Discharge or redeeming a mortgage
Paying off a mortgage.

Commission
The fee charged by estate agents, property consultants, or finders for finding the desired property for a buyer.

Estate Agent
An intermediary between a seller and a buyer who usually works on behalf of the seller.

Fixed interest rate
An interest rate that stays the same throughout the fixed period of the loan, unlike the variable interest rate.

Freehold
Absolute and indefinite ownership of a property.

Fixtures and fittings
A term for all non-structural items included in the sale of a property.

Gazumping
A scenario in which the seller demands more money or accepts a higher offer, just before exchange of contracts.

Gazundering
A situation in which the buyer offers less than the agreed-upon price just before exchange of contracts.

Ground rent
The annual fee that a leaseholder pays to a freeholder.

Home buyer's report
A surveyor's report containing a valuation and details of the condition of the property.

Indemnity premium
An additional charge to cover the lender against higher risk to exposure when a mortgage is say, more than 75% of the property's value.

Land Registry
This is the government department that keeps a record of land ownership in the country.

Land Certificate

A certificate from the Land Registry proving ownership of a property or land.

Negative Equity

The shortfall between the value of a property and the outstanding sum owed on a mortgage.

Offer

The sum of money that the buyer offers to pay for a property.

Sole agency

The choice of a single estate agent to act on the seller's behalf, incurring a lower fee than a multi-agency sale.

Solicitor

A legal expert who handles all documentation for sale and purchase of a property.

Retention

The practice of holding back part of a mortgage loan until repairs to the property are satisfactorily completed.

Private Sale

This refers to the sale of a property without the use of an estate agent as an intermediary.

Registered land
Land for which ownership is registered at the land registry.

Planning permission
This is the permission granted by the local planning authority (usually by the local council) for any new building, major extension, or change of use of a building.

Preliminary enquiries
Questions that the seller must answer before the exchange of contracts.

Redemption penalties
Costs that may be incurred if the borrower repays the loan too early or switches to another lender.

Re-mortgage
The refinancing of a property by switching the mortgage from one lender to another with a new mortgage.

Stamp Duty
A government tax on property purchase ranging from 1 - 4 % of the purchase price for properties above a certain price determined by the government.

Title
The legal ownership of a property or land.

Title Deeds
The legal document assigning ownership of a property or land.

Transfer Deeds
The Land Registry document that transfers legal ownership from seller to buyer.

Surveyor
This is the person who carries out the survey on a property.

Survey
Inspection of a property for any structural damage, dry rot, rising dampness, etc. before the mortgage offer.

Subject to Contract
Term used in a property sale to indicate that an agreement is not yet legally binding.

Tenants
People renting and living in a particular property.

Tenants in common
Property owners who have won unequal shares of a property and are free to dispose of their share in any way they wish.

Under offer
Term applied to a property for which the seller has provisionally accepted the buyer's offer.

Valuation
A surveyor's report required by the lender.

Vendor
The seller of a property or a plot of land.

Multi-Agency
The selection of two or more real estate agents to act on the seller's behalf, incurring a higher fee than if the sale is completed by sole agency.

A List of Useful Contacts

Council of Mortgage Lenders (CML)

This is a not-for-profit organisation and the trade association for the mortgage lending industry, whose members account for around 95% of residential mortgage lending in the UK. These include banks, building societies, and other mortgage lenders. If you need to obtain a mortgage from any of the members in their directory, their contact is as follows:

>Council of Mortgage Lenders,
>Bush House, North West Wing,
>Aldwych, London
>WC2B 4PJ.

>Tel: 0845 373 6771,
>Fax: 0845 373 6778,
>Website: www.cml.org.uk

The Law Society of England & Wales

This is the independent professional body for solicitors. If you are looking for a solicitor to do the conveyance of your house purchase in your local area, they may be contacted at:

>The Law Society of England & Wales,
>The Law Society's Hall,
>113 Chancery Lane,
>London,
>WC2A 1PL.

>Tel: 0207 242 1222,
>Fax: 0207 831 0344,
>Website: www.thelawsociety.org.uk

Timo Real Estate Solutions UK Ltd

If you are a domestic or foreign property investor looking for a reliable property finder, or a company that specialises in sourcing residential and commercial properties in London and throughout the whole of the United Kingdom, the contact details for this company are as follows:

Timo Real Estate Solutions UK Ltd,
London, UK.

Website: www.timorealestatesolutions.co.uk

The Bank of England

This is the central Bank of England and the model on which many modern central banks in the world are based. They have many publications that can offer a lot of insight into the state of the country's economy, which in turn could also prove invaluable to you as you plan to make your property investments or run new business in the United Kingdom.

>Bank of England,
>Threadneedle St,
>London, EC2R 8AH.

>Tel: 0207 601 4878,
>Fax: 0207 601 4771,
>E-mail: enquiries@bankofengland.co.uk
>Website: www.bankofengland.co.uk

Acknowledgements

I would like to express my sincere and deepest gratitude to the many people who have played a significant part in shaping my destiny over the years, and most importantly recently as I struggled with all sorts of issues whilst writing this book and getting my business off the ground

(www.timorealestatesolutions.co.uk).

As a matter of fact, I have dreamt of writing a book (not particularly a business book, just any book) for more than twenty years. For one reason or another, I knew I had to get on with it, but I always found excuses not to, whether my career, parental duties, or financial constraints. It was not until early this year when I met Ms Clare Turner-Marshall, someone whom I am immensely proud to call my good friend and mentor, that I thought to myself that this is it ... either I write the book now or go to my grave a very miserable, grumpy man. I decided on the former and immediately started this journey. I would not even have taken the first steps of doing this project, however, if it wasn't for the belief that Clare had in me. Believe it or not, after you have had so many knocks, rejections, disappointments, and other some failures over a long period and then someone comes to you and says, "I do believe in you, and I know that you can achieve all your goals in life, not in five but in three years' time!" you really feel like a very big burden has been lifted off your shoulders, and out of the blue, I slowly began to think that yes, I could really dare to dream again!

Basically, I had been in a dark place, but because Clare gave me a lot of positive energy, advice, guidance, and support, I started not only to get my new business off the ground but also started to write this business book with a lot of confidence and sheer determination. Apologies Clare that I did not initially tell you that I was actually writing this book, but take it from me that all the credit for this project goes to you! It is you who have made this happen. I am not going to say much about this for now because I know you are very likely to reject any credit for any of this due to your humility. The fact of the matter is: if it weren't for Clare, you would certainly not be reading this book. Just for the record – until I leave this world, I will always be so grateful to Clare for being my "guardian angel." I will always love you for giving me a chance in life when no one else had any time for me.

Equally important is the invaluable contribution to this project by Ms Stephanie Hale. Without her invaluable advice, guidance, and support, I would still be carrying this dream of having my book published in my head. Basically, all the credit for the choice of diction, tone, target readership, audience, title, typesetting, book cover, to mention a few things in this book, goes to her. As an expert and an author in her own right, her tireless mentoring efforts, advice, guidance, and support are what have enabled me to have this end-product: a simple and inspirational book which provides all the relevant information without any jargon to any aspiring property investor, entrepreneur, or developer out there who genuinely wants to know the basics about the property industry. I remain so grateful indeed to all of you; thank you ever so much for everything.

There are many other people who unbeknownst to them have also been so helpful to me whilst doing this project. Without going into the details, I would also like to use this opportunity to thank Gobnait Cronin, Carol Rhona Mukasa Kayemba (you took a chance on me big time!), Elizabeth Kibalama (Omuzukukulu owo mulembe), Gail Powell, Ben Galley, Claudia Watson, Louise Defty; Segun Osinaike for sharing vital business information with me; Charmaine Tesaga (for the great and invaluable moral support), Lisa Jeffs (for daring to dream the big dream with me ... We will get there. No doubt!!!), Ibrahim, D Hirani, Robert M Kasirye, Anil Hirani, Katasi Eva, Tracey Mackenzie (for the brilliant hard talk), John Mbuga, David Kamuzze, Gobnait Jessica Wallus and Ali Mutebi, Maama Norah, Maama Irene, Lisa Cousins, Charles Mukasa, William Mpalanyi, the late Charles Karegyesa, Uncle Richard and Auntie Robinah Golola as well as Jessica, Solome, Jackie and "Prince Omuzukulu", Duncan and Miriam Neville, Lynn, David and Eliza; the three ladies at Kirsty's school, namely Janet, Carol and Vicky for the laughs; Mrs Rachael Dickinson (Kirsty's teacher) as well as the lovely folks I share a smile with on the different WhatsApp groups to which I belong, Trevor Mealham and Stuart Larsky for those long telephone chats; Sara Vitkauskas in Dubai "for business matters"; Nichola Lewis Jones for simply being real and cool; David Wheaton, Toni Hagon, Vince Thomas, Heather Pope, Jean, Liz, Tracey and Fuhara Ahsan at my local library for the print-outs, smiles, and of course "time"; Mr and Mrs Kupoluyi, Samar Al Obaidy, Bishop Trevor Mwamba, Joy Lubega, Charlotte Turp for volunteering to be the first person to buy this book), our neighbours Mr Godfrey and Mrs Irene Sekisonge and Salongo George and Nalongo Tina with all their families ... all of whom have indirectly or unconsciously been of much support to me and my family.

At a personal level, I must also point out the great sacrifice that my parents, my dad and mum (Miima, as she was fondly known ... may her beautiful soul rest in eternal peace), put in to raise me and my siblings. As you can imagine, Uganda, where I originally come from is really gifted in nature, and one of the most beautiful places in the world, but ironically also one of the hardest places to grow up. I still do not know how my parents managed to put food on the table day in, day out and still send us to school ... a miracle, in my opinion! The truth of the matter is that without their hard work and moral guidance, I would simply not be where I am today, and for that I will always remain so grateful. I simply cannot forget to mention Mr Godfrey and Mrs Miriam Kavuma who first inspired me to be whatever I wanted to be in life by being the closest real-life example to what success in life is all about. Another benefactor is the late Mrs Veronica Mpagi, for whom words fail to describe how she literally gave me that sense of direction from time to time, especially during my teenage years and early adulthood. May her soul rest in eternal peace. Another big role model of mine is the late Dr James Mulwana for his great humility despite the trappings of power, influence, and immense wealth. I only saw him once at a public gathering, and I still regret why I did not approach him to pick his brain about running a business successfully. I did learn from him and Mr Kavuma the "proper skills and qualifications from the University of Life." My humble wish is to be just like them, that is, to be so wealthy but remain so down-to-earth and approachable. Other notable role models to me who have had a great influence on my life include Nelson Mandela, Tony Blair, and Margaret Thatcher for their different but exemplary leadership skills; Michael Jackson for his unique and exceptional talent; Mahatma Gandhi, Winston Churchill, and Barack Obama for their oratory skills and inspirational lives. In terms of self-help development and character building, I have borrowed a leaf or two from a lot of these people's life stories, and I do feel that I am what I am today because of the lessons I have taken from them. Moreover, I also want to thank my dearest family including Dorian, Cathy, Ruth, Ezra, Rita, Titti, Andrew, Kawuma, Phillip, Moses, Hannington, Esther, "Maama Christine" as well as the relatives, and friends who have been there for me all these years. I am sorry that I have not mentioned all of you here this time, as it would take me days if not weeks to do so.

Please allow me to also express my sincerest gratitude to Olivia Muwanguzi for all the love and sacrifice for putting up with me, not only during this project. I have been using your laptop and Kirsty's iPad to do this and not once have both of you complained about monopolising your gadgets. Your patience, understanding, and support have been invaluable. I just hope that this book makes you as proud as I am since we have gone through so many trials and tribulations together. I do believe that despite all the odds, this book is truly mine, yours, and Kirsty's great achievement!

And finally, to all of you: my readers, business associates, and clients who continue to support my literary work and business so enthusiastically.

Thank you so, so much.

www.timoseks.com

www.ingramcontent.com/pod-product-compliance
Lightning Source LLC
Chambersburg PA
CBHW020652220526
45464CB00001B/402